FIND 'EM FAST

A PRIVATE INVESTIGATOR'S WORKBOOK

JOHN D. McCANN

PALADIN PRESS
BOULDER, COLORADO

Find 'Em Fast
A Private Investigator's Workbook
by John D. McCann
Copyright © 1984 by John D. McCann

ISBN 0-87364-301-1
Printed in the United States of America

Published by Paladin Press, a division of
Paladin Enterprises, Inc., P.O. Box 1307,
Boulder, Colorado 80306, USA.
(303) 443-7250

Direct inquiries and/or orders to the above address.

TABLE OF CONTENTS

Chapter 1.   INTRODUCTION   1

Chapter 2.   BACKGROUND AND PREEMPLOYMENT
             INVESTIGATION   3
                  Background Investigations
                  Preemployment Investigations
                  Employment Applications

Chapter 3.   MISSING PERSONS 13

Chapter 4.   SURVEILLANCE AND TAILING 23
                  Preparation
                  Tailing Basics
                  Single Investigator Foot Tail
                  Multiple Investigator Foot Tail
                  Mobile Tailing
                  Stake-Out

Chapter 5.   CIVIL LITIGATION 38
                  Automobile Accident Investigation
                  Public Accident Investigation
                  Product Liability Investigation

Chapter 6.   INTERVIEWS AND STATEMENTS 48
                  Interviews
                  Statements

Chapter 7.   UNDERCOVER ASSIGNMENTS 56
                  Selection and Screening
                  Preparation for Assignment
                  Working Undercover

Chapter 8.   INVESTIGATIVE PHOTOGRAPHY 60
                  Equipment
                  Purpose of Photography
                  Methods of Photography

Chapter 9.   REPORTS 67

Chapter 10. YOUR OWN AGENCY 75

Appendix 1. SOURCES OF INFORMATION 87

Appendix 2. INVESTIGATOR ASSOCIATIONS 130

Appendix 3. CORRESPONDENCE SCHOOLS 133

Appendix 4. CODE OF ETHICS 134

Appendix 5. INDEX TO FORMS 135

DEDICATION

This manual is dedicated to Sue, for her encouragement ("You'll finish it someday"), assistance ("I'm typing, I'm typing!") and patience ("Would you please come to bed!");

                              and

My mother and father who always say, "This is our son, he's a ... what kind of work is it you do again?".

SPECIAL THANKS

I give special thanks to Gene Daley, who gave me my start and used to always say, "No you can't have a raise!";

                              and

Joseph Alercia II, who is not only a fine private investigator, but a very close friend and confidant;

                              and

Ted Losee, for his help, support, friendship and being there when you need a true friend.

Chapter-1

INTRODUCTION

Todays private investigator must constantly represent himself as a professional who operates in a thorough, decisive, and methodical manner. The image of the private investigator in the past has been rather poor. Reasons for this range from shoddy and incompetent services by poor quality and nonprofessional private investigators to the misrepresentation by television and movies which portray the private investigator as an uneducated and bungling gumshoe.

For reasons such as these, there is no longer any room in the private investigation field for persons not willing to be a professional. Once a private investigator realizes that he or she is in a highly competitive field, where only the professional survives, he or she will be more than willing to study, learn, and acquire all the knowledge that is available and necessary to function in todays specialized and technical society.

In any professional field today, it is becoming more important to have a "ready reference" to utilize as a refresher for knowledge already possessed, and as a supplement to augment this basic knowledge. This manual was written for the professional private investigator for use as a "ready reference", and for the novice investigator, as a study guide. Besides containing an abundance of material of benefit to the professional investigator as well as the novice, it also contains a multitude of check-lists and example blank forms which can be utilized to assist in making the work of a private investigator easier, less time consuming, and more cost effective. "An investigators time and advice are his stock in trade."[1] This means that an investigator should never waste time, but always give professional advice. This manual provides the basis for both.

---

[1] Quotation taken from the book "JAY J. ARMES INVESTIGATOR, AS TOLD TO FREDERICK NOLAN".

Chapter - 2

BACKGROUND AND PREEMPLOY-MENT INVESTIGATIONS

On many occasions a private investigator will receive a request to perform an investigation in regards to an individuals' background or to check and verify information supplied by an applicant on an employment application.

BACKGROUND INVESTIGATIONS

When initiating a background investigation, all available information at hand should be checked for accuracy. This would include such apparently trivial information as names, addresses, telephone numbers, dates of births, etc. On many occasions, the information accumulated during an extensive investigation was found to be useless because of an error in the original data which caused an inaccurate course to be taken by an investigator.

After verifying the initial information, an investigator should check all available public records for information and data in regard to the person being investigated. Oftentimes, the amount of information obtained from these sources is plentiful and can be used, on many occasions, to help construct a composite picture of a person.

During the course of a background investigation it is sometimes necessary for an investigator to interview relatives, friends, fellow employees, past employers, or anyone that may enlighten the investigator in regard to the person being investigated. However, when questioning such persons, it is sometimes desirable to ask the questions under pretext so that an honest answer is obtained. Many times, if a person knows that a private investigator is asking the questions, they will tend to bend the truth or refuse to talk. There are innumerable pretexts which can be utilized to extract information in this manner. The following are only a couple of the many which can be conceived by a clever investigator.

When desiring to obtain information in regard to what a person does for a living, or trying to uncover whether a person is working, the following pretext is often useful. The investigator would approach a friend or neighbor of the person being investigated and introduce himself as an employee of a local finance company. The investigator would continue by explaining that he is trying to verify some information that was placed on a loan application by their friend (or neighbor depending on who the investigator is talking to). This introduction allows the investigator to ask a full range of questions about the person under investigation without making anyone suspicious of the reason for questioning. By using the pretext of only trying to verify a loan application, a person being asked the questions may feel as though they are helping their friend or neighbor and will usually be very talkative.

Another pretext which oftentimes elicits valuable information for the investigator is the "consumer auto insurance survey". The investigator draws up a fake survey and introduces himself as an employee of a private firm which is

doing a survey in order to determine if the insurance rates
for the area are too high. Most people love to save money
and will be more than happy to answer questions if they feel
it may help to lower their insurance rates. This type of
pretext can actually be used on the person being investigated,
or their family. Questions such as, how many persons are in
the family, how many drive, and how many work, etc. can be
asked without the investigator appearing to be over curious
or prying. When the list of pretext questions is made up, the
investigator can interlace questions he actually wants answers
to between questions that appear trivial and are easily an-
swered. An example of this type of pretext survey follows this
chapter.

It must be understood that not all the information obtained by means of pretext can be considered fact. However,
the information is useful in verifying data which is suspect-
ed of being correct.

PREEMPLOYMENT INVESTIGATIONS

When conducting a preemployment investigation, it is
extremely important to verify all information received on the
employment application. No information on the employment application should be considered fact until a thorough verification has been made by an investigator.

When reviewing the past employment history of the applicant, all time gaps of two or more months of nonemployment
should be noted and a reasonable explanation obtained from
the applicant. The veracity of these explanations should also

be verified through investigation. A background investigation should be conducted on all applicants as well, being especially attentive to the possibility of a past criminal record. If possible, the investigator should interview past employers in order to verify reasons stated for leaving, by the applicant. The investigator should also determine if the past employer would be willing to rehire the former employee if a position was available. Sometimes a former employer will give a reason for leaving which will enable the past employee to get another job, but is not the actual truth. If the former employer states he would not be willing to rehire the past employee, it may be indicative that the true reason for leaving was other than the stated one.

EMPLOYMENT APPLICATIONS

An employment application should be designed in order for the employer to obtain as much information as possible from the applicant. The larger the quantity of information received from the applicant initially, the more the investigator has to work with.

All employment applications should end with a statement that certifies that the foregoing statements are true and correct to the best of the applicants' knowledge and belief. This should be followed by a statement in which the applicant acknowledged that they understand that if they have given any false or misleading information, it could result in their immediate termination from employment. This statement should be immediately followed by a space for the applicant to write in the date and place their signature.

Following this chapter is an example of an employment application. It collects the type of information which will help an investigator during his investigation of the applicant.

PRETEXT SURVEY

CONSUMER AUTO INSURANCE RESEARCH SURVEY

1) How many persons are in the family?

2) How many cars are in the family?

3) How many drivers are in the family?

4) How many members of the family are under the age of 25?

5) How many members of the family are under the age of 18?

6) How many are employed?

7) Type of work they are employed at?

8) Where are they employed?

9) How long employed there?

10) Do they drive to work?

11) How many miles are driven to work?

12) Full time or part time?

13) Type and year of car owned?

14) Any accidents in the last 5 years?

15) How many get a safe drivers rate?

16) Have any attended a drivers education course?

17) Type of insurance carried?

Application For Employment

Applicants are considered for all positions without regard to race, color, religion, sex, national origin, age, marital or veteran status, or the presence of a non-job-related medical condition or handicap.

(PLEASE PRINT)

Date of Application _____

Position(s) Applied For _____

Referral Source: ☐ Advertisement   ☐ Friend   ☐ Relative   ☐ Walk-In

☐ Employment Agency   ☐ Other _____

Name _____
LAST   FIRST   MIDDLE

Address _____
NUMBER   STREET   CITY   STATE   ZIP CODE

Telephone (____) _____ Social Security Number _____
Area Code

If employed and you are under 18,
can you furnish a work permit?   ☐ Yes   ☐ No

Have you filed an application here before?   ☐ Yes   ☐ No   If Yes, give date _____

Have you ever been employed here before?   ☐ Yes   ☐ No   If Yes, give date _____

Are you employed now?   ☐ Yes   ☐ No   May we contact your present employer?   ☐ Yes   ☐ No

Are you prevented from lawfully becoming employed
in this country because of Visa or Immigration Status?   ☐ Yes   ☐ No
(Proof of citizenship or immigration status
may be required upon employment.)

On what date would you be available for work? _____

Are you available to work   ☐ Full Time   ☐ Part-Time   ☐ Shift Work   ☐ Temporary

Are you on a lay-off and subject to recall?   ☐ Yes   ☐ No

Can you travel if a job requires it?   ☐ Yes   ☐ No

Have you been convicted of a felony within the last 7 years?   ☐ No   ☐ Yes

If Yes, please explain _____

Veteran of the U.S. military service? ☐ Yes ☐ No   If Yes, Branch _____

Do you have any physical, mental or medical impairment
or disability that would limit your job performance
for the position for which you are applying?   ☐ Yes ☐ No

If Yes, please explain _____

Are there workplace accommodations which
would assure better job placement and/or enable you to
perform your job to your maximum capability?   ☐ Yes ☐ No

If Yes, please indicate: _____

Indicate what foreign languages you speak, read, and/or write.

	FLUENTLY	GOOD	FAIR
SPEAK			
READ			
WRITE			

List professional, trade, business or civic activities and offices held.
(Exclude those which indicate race, color, religion, sex or national origin): _____

_____

_____

Give name, address and telephone number of three references who are not related to you and are not
previous employers.

_____

_____

_____

Special Employment Notice to Disabled Veterans, Vietnam Era Veterans, and Individuals With
Physical Or Mental Handicaps.

Government contractors are subject to Section 402 of the Vietnam Era Veterans Readjustment Act of 1974 which
requires that they take affirmative action to employ and advance in employment qualified disabled veterans and
veterans of the Vietnam Era, and Section 503 of the Rehabilitation Act of 1973, as amended, which requires
government contractors to take affirmative action to employ and advance in employment qualified handicapped
individuals.

If you are a disabled veteran, or have a physical or mental handicap, you are invited to volunteer this information.
The purpose is to provide information regarding proper placement and appropriate accommodation to enable
you to perform the job in a proper and safe manner. This information will be treated as confidential. Failure to
provide this information will not jeopardize or adversely affect any consideration you may receive for
employment.

If you wish to be identified, please sign below.

☐ Handicapped Individual   ☐ Disabled Veteran   ☐ Vietnam Era Veteran

Signed _____

Employment Experience

Start with your present or last job. Include military service assignments and volunteer activities. Exclude organization names which indicate race, color, religion, sex or national origin.

1	Employer	Dates Employed		Work Performed
		From	To	
	Address			
	Job Title	Hourly Rate/Salary		
		Starting	Final	
	Supervisor			
	Reason for Leaving			
2	Employer	Dates Employed		Work Performed
		From	To	
	Address			
	Job Title	Hourly Rate/Salary		
		Starting	Final	
	Supervisor			
	Reason for Leaving			
3	Employer	Dates Employed		Work Performed
		From	To	
	Address			
	Job Title	Hourly Rate/Salary		
		Starting	Final	
	Supervisor			
	Reason for Leaving			
4	Employer	Dates Employed		Work Performed
		From	To	
	Address			
	Job Title	Hourly Rate/Salary		
		Starting	Final	
	Supervisor			
	Reason for Leaving			

If you need additional space, please continue on a separate sheet of paper.

Special Skills and Qualifications

Summarize special skills and qualifications
acquired from employment or other experience _____

_____

_____

_____

Education

	Elementary	High	College/University	Graduate/ Professional
School Name				
Years Completed: (Circle)	4 5 6 7 8	9 10 11 12	1 2 3 4	1 2 3 4
Diploma/Degree				
Describe Course Of Study:				

Describe Specialized Training, Apprenticeship, Skills, and Extra-Curricular Activities	

Honors Received:

State any additional information you feel may be helpful to us in considering your application.

Agreement

I certify that answers given herein are true and complete to the best of my knowledge.

I authorize investigation of all statements contained in this application for employment as may be necessary in arriving at an employment decision.

In the event of employment, I understand that false or misleading information given in my application or interview(s) may result in discharge. I understand, also, that I am required to abide by all rules and regulations of the Company.

_____   _____
Signature of Applicant   Date

For Personnel Department Use Only

Arrange Interview ☐ Yes ☐ No

Remarks _____

_____
                                                                    INTERVIEWER   DATE

Employed ☐ Yes ☐ No   Date of Employment _____

Job Title _____   Hourly Rate/ Salary _____ Department _____

          By _____
                                    NAME AND TITLE   DATE

Chapter-3

MISSING PERSONS

One of the most interesting and challenging cases an investigator can receive is a missing persons investigation. This type of case can also be difficult. Not every person that is supposed to be "missing" is missing. Most missing persons are not actually lost. They know exactly where they are. The problem arises when the client doesn't know where the missing person is.

This is where the investigator comes in. Sometimes a person that is supposed to be missing is actually hiding in an attempt to conceal their whereabouts. On other occasions, a missing person is merely an old friend or relative who has moved away without leaving a forwarding address and a client wishes them located.

An investigator should initiate a missing persons investigation by collecting as much information and data available on the person missing. A blank data sheet can be made up and used for the purpose of ensuring that all available information has been accumulated (an example of a missing person report follows this chapter).

The longer a person has been missing, the easier they are to find. Old habits are hard to break and it is usually difficult for any person to just completely stop communication with family or old friends. This is where patience and an investigators expertise really shows itself.

An investigator should start at the beginning; and that

is the missing persons back yard. Talk to neighbors and friends to see if they have heard anything that might give you a lead. Check with the local post office to see if the missing person has applied for a change of address. This is often an overlooked detail. Talk with present and former employers and employees. If the missing person belonged to any trade or labor unions or fraternity clubs or organizations, check with them. Talk to creditors, insurance agents and credit bureaus. If the missing person was a drinker, check with bartenders at bars the person frequented. Check with the motor vehicle bureau to determine if a change of address had been made. On occasion, a missing person has been found by simply checking the telephone book or city directory.

An investigator should leave no stone unturned and should follow every lead. Put yourself in the persons position. If you were them, where would you go? Do they have a living relative in another state? An old school chum? Work on a possible theory or devise a plausible scenario. Then follow your leads. Sometimes it takes alot of perserverance and maybe even a little luck, but if the missing person is still living, they can be found!

MISSING PERSON REPORT

DATE: _____ CLIENT: _____

PERSONAL

Name:(Last) _____ (First) _____ (Middle) __

S.S.#:_____ Citizen _____ Alias: _____

Address: _____ Phone: _____

Age: _____ D.O.B.: _____ Race: _____ Sex: _____

Occupation:_____ Employer:_____

Address: _____ Phone: _____

Probable Destination: _____

Possible cause of absence: _____

Date & time last seen: _____ Time reported:_____

Last seen at: _____

Car:(Year) _____ (Make) _____ (Model) _____

(Doors) _____ (Color) _____ (Lic.Plate #) _____

(Condition) _____

Driver's Lic. #:_____ _____ Type:_____

Driving records (Accidents & Citations): _____

_____

Legal Owner:_____ Address: _____

_____ Auto Ins.Co.:_____

_____ Address: _____

Balance owed on car:_____To who: _____

PHYSICAL (Note peculiarities)

Height:_____Weight:_____Build:_____Complexion:_____

Eyes:_____Glasses:_____Contact lenses:_____

Hair:_____Part:_____Length:_____Moustache:_____

MISSING PERSON REPORT (CONT)-2

Beard: _____ Sideburns: _____ Teeth: _____ False: _____

Ears: _____ Eyebrows: _____ Accent: _____

Sensual defects: _____

Deformities: _____

Scars: _____

Birthmarks: _____ Moles: _____

Tattoo marks: _____

Condition(Mental): _____

(Physical): _____

Under M.D.or D.D.S. care: _____

Special diet: _____

Necessary medicines: _____

R. or L. handed: _____ Narcotics used: _____

Smoke: _____ Brand: _____ Drink: _____

Characteristics, Habits, Mannerisms: _____

_____

_____

Hangouts: _____

_____

Clothing(Last seen wearing): _____

_____

Briefcase: _____ Jewelry: _____

Other clothing taken: _____

_____

_____

Pawnable possessions taken: _____

_____

_____

BACKGROUND

Place of Birth:_____Religion:_____

Father's Name:_____D.O.B.: _____

Nativity:_____Father's present address:_____

_____Occupation:_____

Employer & address:_____

Mother's maiden name:_____D.O.B.:_____

Nativity:_____Mother's present address:_____

_____Occupation:_____

Employer & address: _____

Brothers & Sisters (Address, D.O.B.,Occupation):_____

_____

_____

_____

Other Relatives (Address & Occupation):_____

_____

_____

_____

Martital Status:_____Spouse's Name:_____

Address:_____

Occupation:_____Employer:_____

Employers address:_____

D.O.B.:_____Nativity:_____

Children (Names, D.O.B.,Nativity,Where now):_____

_____

_____

_____

_____

Former Spouse:_____D.O.B.:_____

Address:_____

Nativity:_____Occupation:_____

Employer & address:_____

Alimony:_____How much:_____How sent:_____

Subject's Employer:_____

Address:_____

Former Occupations:_____

Former Employers & Address:_____

_____

_____

_____

_____

Friends & Associates & Address:_____

_____

_____

_____

_____

Grade School:_____

Address:_____

High School:_____

Address:_____

College:_____

Address:_____

Degree:_____Year:_____

Correspondence Schools:_____

_____

_____

Places visited:_____

_____

_____

_____

Languages spoken:_____

Countries visited:_____

_____

Former Addresses:_____

_____

_____

_____

Hobbies:_____

_____

Organizations & Clubs:_____

_____

_____

FINANCIAL

Bank:_____ Branch:_____

Address:_____

Checking Amount:_____ Savings Amount:_____

Contents of safety Deposit box:_____

_____

Other Banks:_____

_____

_____

Credit Cards:_____

_____

_____

Money owed to subject:_____

By whom:_____

Amount in debt:_____

To whom:_____

On unemployment:_____How long:_____

Stock Broker:_____

Address:_____

Amount of stocks:_____

Amount of Bonds:_____

C.P.A.:_____

Address:_____

Insurance Agent:_____

Address:_____

Attorney:_____

Address:_____

Realtor:_____

Address:_____

Phone, Water, Gas deposits:_____

_____

Car financed by:_____

Address:_____

Pension or Relief:_____

Other Income:_____

_____

RECORDS

Ever finger printed:_____When:_____Where:_____

Why:_____

Classification (If known):_____

Police Record:_____When:_____

Where:_____

Crime:_____

Disposition of case:_____

Prison:_____Time served:_____

Crime:_____

Parole Records:_____Parole Officer:_____

Address:_____

Mental Hospitals:_____

Pistol Permit:_____When:_____Where:_____

Why:_____

Make:_____Caliber:_____Serial No.:_____

Make:_____Caliber:_____Serial No.:_____

Other Weapons:_____

Warrants Outstanding:_____

Passports:_____Visas:_____

Laundry Marks:_____Cleaning Marks:_____

Pets:_____Descriptions:_____

_____Names:_____

Veterinarian:_____Address:_____

_____Pet Clubs:_____

Hunting and/or Fishing Lic.:_____

Armed Service Branch:_____Rank:_____

Date In:_____Date Out:_____Discharge Type:_____

_____Specializations:_____

_____

Veteran Organizations:_____

Registered Voter:_____Where:_____

P.O. Forwarding: _____

Unions: _____

MISC.

Where do you think subject is: _____

Explain: _____

_____

Is there anyone the subject would or might be corresponding with?:

_____

Any relatives or friends contacted: _____

Authorities notified:Police:_____ D.A.:_____ F.B.I.:_____

Other: _____

Previously missing:_____ When:_____ Why:_____

Reported By:_____Phone:_____

Address: _____

Will you accept a collect telephone call if we need more informa-

tion:_____.

DETAILS AND REMARKS

_____

_____

_____

_____

_____

_____

_____

_____

_____

_____

_____

Chapter - 4

SURVEILLANCE AND TAILING

Surveillance is the careful and continuous watching of something or someone, carried on in a secretive or discrete manner, in order to obtain information in regards to the identities or activities of a subject or subjects. Surviellance's can be broken down into two general catagories. The first is whereby the investigator must move, either by foot or vehicle, in order to follow a subject or subjects. This type of surveillance is called "tailing". The second is whereby the investigator remains in a fixed position to observe a subject or subjects, and is called a "stake-out".

PREPARATION

Thorough preparation should be an investigators first objective when starting any surveillance. Before any surveillance is initiated, it is imperative that all data received in regards to the subject or subjects at the beginning of the surveillance be verified for accuracy. Take nothing for granted, as many a surveillance was a failure, and the time expended lost, because the initial data was incorrect.

Whenever possible, an investigator should make a thorough survey of the area the surveillance will, or is likely to, involve. This will allow the investigator to become familiar with the avenues of approach, departure, and overall topography. If a residence is to be staked

23

out for the purpose of watching a subject who is supposed to reside there, the investigator had better verify positively that the said subject does so in fact.

During all phases of any type of surveillance, descriptions of all subjects should be noted and recorded, and extensive notes of all movements, occurences, or events, also recorded with accuracy for future use. All such information will be invaluable later in adding credibility to the investigators stated observations. Whenever possible, photographs or video tape recordings should be taken to supplement and aid in verifying observations.

TAILING BASICS

As stated previsouly, tailing is whereby the investigator must follow a subject by foot or vehicle. When tailing a subject there are certain rules and specific procedures which should be followed in order for the investigator to be successful. The first rule is the "cardinal rule". It is better to lose a subject than to burn a subject. To burn a subject is to let the subject know positively that they are being tailed. It is imperative that an investigator always remember that if the subject is lost, they can be found again at another time. However, once a subject knows they are being followed, the subject is burned, and will be almost impossible to follow. The subject will become what is known as "surveillance conscious", and attempt by any means, to thwart the investigators effort at tailing them. Even if the case is not ruined, the investigator who burned the subject can never follow that subject again, and a new investigator must be assigned to the case.

Whenever tailing a subject, an investigator should always avoid attracting attention to himself, and should act and move in a smooth and inconspicuous manner. An investigator should attempt to fit into the environment in which he is working by wearing clothes that make him appear as though he belongs in that area. If an investigator is tailing a subject in a lower social economic area, a three piece suit would not be appropriate. An investigator should never wear a disguise such as a false beard, hair, etc.. If an investigator wishes to change his appearance, it will suffice to do so by means such as taking off or putting on a hat, removing or putting on a jacket or coat, removing a tie, or wearing glasses. It must be remembered that an investigator should avoid doing anything out of the ordinary. Movements such as jumping behind corners, or peeking from behind light poles could draw attention to an investigator and possibly cause a subject to become suspicious of a tail.

An investigator should always carry proper identification and sufficient funds in cash and credit cards. If a subject decides to enter a restaurant, jump on a bus, or board a plane, an investigator will have to be in a position, financially, to follow.

SINGLE INVESTIGATOR FOOT TAIL

The single investigator foot tail is the most difficult to perform. Whenever an investigator is tailing a
subject on foot by himself, he should never take his mind
off the subject in an attempt to maintain constant observance of the subject. If an investigator allows his
mind to wander from the subject for a mere moment, the
investigator may find that he no longer has a subject to
tail. If for some reason a subject is lost, the investigator should check all the subjects' known hangouts in an
attempt to relocate the subject. If the subject cannot
be relocated then the investigator should return to the
place the subject was tailed from and wait there for the
subject to return.

When foot tailing a subject, an investigator should
attempt to keep as much distance between himself and the
subject as possible and still be able to maintain good
observation. If foot tailing on a busy city sidewalk,
and the sidewalks are crowded, the distance between the
investigator and subject will have to be maintained
fairly close. However, if the sidewalks are sparsely
populated, the investigator had better lag back. When
possible, an investigator should attempt to parallel the
subject from the sidewalk on the opposite side of the
street.

An investigator should be extremely careful when a
subject walks around a corner. A suspicious subject has
been known to walk around a corner and then stop in an

attempt to discover if they are being tailed. If an investigator came hurriedly around a corner in an attempt to maintain observance, he could be burned by the subject. In a situation such as this, it would be wiser for an investigator to walk straight past the corner and glance in the direction the subject turned. If the subject is still walking, and does not appear to be suspicious of a tail, the investigator can continue.

If a subject should enter a restaurant, the investigator should not enter immediately. It should first be determined if the subject might not have entered only to buy cigarettes or possibly to use the rest room. When the investigator does enter, he should locate the subject and position himself at a table which will allow the investigator maximum visibility of the subject and exits. The investigator should always attempt to pay for his meal when ordering it. By doing this, the investigator can leave immediately if the subject gets up suddenly to pay for their check. This allows the investigator to be waiting outside when the subject exits.

If a subject gets on a bus, the investigator should attempt to board the same bus, positioning himself behind the subject if possible. If the investigator cannot follow the subject onto the bus without appearing suspicious, then he should either follow the bus in a taxi, or have a taxi hurry the investigator to the next bus stop, whereupon the investigator can board the bus at that time.

At any time during a foot tail, if the subject ever

approaches the investigator and confronts him with "are you following me?", the investigator should always deny, deny, deny. Never under any circumstances admit to a subject that they are being tailed. If a subject stops all of a sudden and turns around, the investigator should never panic. Because a subject stops and turns, does not always mean they are suspicious. The subject might have decided to go to a place they have gone past, or change direction. In a case where a subject does this, the investigator should continue walking past the subject and then, while stopping to look into a store window, glance back, relocate the subject, and continue the tail. An investigator should always avoid direct eye contact with a subject, but should never avoid looking in the subjects direction.

MULTIPLE INVESTIGATOR FOOT TAIL

The multiple investigator foot tail is performed by two or more investigators at the same time. The multiple investigator foot tail is advisable when a subject is to be tailed in a crowded city, or when a subject is possibly surveillance suspicious. Surveillance suspicious does not mean the subject knows they are being tailed, only that the subject may suspect that they are being tailed. Persons who are involved in illegal activities or activities that may upset a spouse or friend are oftentimes automatically surveillance suspicious.

Two or more investigators can tail a subject with

less exposure to each investigator than can one. When
tailing a subject, each investigator should attempt to
stay withing visual contact of each other whenever possible. An investigator should never yell to another investigator when tailing a subject. In order for one
investigator to communicate with another, some type of
signals should be devised prior to a tail being initiated.
Again, it should be mentioned that an investigator should
never move or act in any manner that could draw attention
to himself. When devising signals to be used on a tail,
they should be casual in manner. The lighting of a
cigarette, the folding of a newspaper and placing it
under an arm, or the taking off of a pair of glasses,
could all appear as a natural movement by an observer.
However, each could be pre-designated to mean something
special to an investigator when tailing.

When two or more investigators are tailing a subject,
one investigator should attempt to remain behind the
subject. The second investigator should parallel the
subject from across the street, and the other investigator
would lag behind the first investigator. In this manner.
if the subject turned a corner, the first investigator,
tailing directly behind the subject, could continue
straight. The second or third investigator would then
pick up the tail on the subject as first investigator. The
investigator who continued straight would then pick up the
position of either the second or third investigator depending
on which one followed the subject.

Another method of the multiple investigator tail is the leap-frog method. When using this method, the investigators continually change their position so the same investigator is not behind the subject continuously. The investigator immediately behind the subject could cross the street and parallel the subject while the investigator lagging behind the subject moves up. The investigator originally paralleling the subject could drop back, cross the street, and lag behind the new first investigator.

A twenty-four hour a day answering service should always be available when on a multiple investigator tail. In this way, if an investigator should become separated from the other investigators, he can call the answering service and inform them of his location and, if possible, a phone number at which he can be reached. Once the other investigators realize that the separated investigator is no longer present, they can call the answering service to determine if the separated investigator has called in. The answering service can then give the location of the investigators to the separated investigator if a phone number was left with them. If not, the answering service can tell the investigators the location of the separated investigator.

MOBILE TAILING

The mobile tailing of a subject is conducted in essentially the same manner as a foot tail with the addition of a vehicle for the investigator and subject. Before initiating a mobile tail, an investigator should always

30

ensure that the vehicle in which he will conduct the tail
has a full tank of gas. In most cases, if an investigator
starts a mobile tail with a full tank of gas, the subject
will need to stop for gas before the investigator. An
inspection of the vehicle should also be conducted prior to
a tail to ensure that the vehicle is in a safe operating
condition. The vehicle should also be equipped with a
good spare tire.

When selecting a vehicle for tailing purposes, it
should always be of a neutral color, such as tan or beige,
and of an unpretentious style. Whenever possible, the
vehicle should be rented or leased. A switch panel should
be constructed for owned vehicles for manual operation of
the headlights, parking lights, overhead interior lights,
and brake lights, from the dashboard. This switch panel
will enable the investigator to turn out one headlight at
a time which will give the vehicle a different appearance
from a rear view mirror. The same effect is achieved when
the parking lights are on or off. The best time to utilize
these switches are after a subject turns a corner. Before
the investigator turns after the subject, he utilizes one
of the light switches which makes the subject think that a
different vehicle is now behind them. The switch for the
overhead interior light is used before an investigator gets
out of his vehicle at night. In this manner, the subject
will not know when the investigator opens his door or be
able to see the investigator when he does. The switch for
the brake lights is utilized so the brake lights can be

31

turned off when an investigator sits with his vehicle in drive, the lights out, and his foot on the brake pedal. This way the brake lights will not shine and give away the investigators position.

Two-way mobile radio communication should be available in all tail vehicles so that investigators can be in constant communication with each other, If there is any other agency or firm on the radio frequency, some type of code should be devised so that communication between investigators cannot be understood by any other persons. However, whenever possible, a radio frequency for private use by the investigators is the best way to go.

Whenever on a mobile tail, there should always be an attempt made to have two investigators for each vehicle. This will allow one investigator to operate the vehicle while the other investigator operates the two-way mobile radio, keep notes, and be available to get out of the vehicle to follow a subject by foot, if necessary, without having to park the vehicle first.

An investigator must always keep in mind that he is not a commissioned police officer, and so must adhere to all traffic laws. Speeding while on a mobile tail is especially difficult to resist when a subject being tailed happens to be a speed demon. However, the investigators drivers license is more important than the loss of a subject. Remember that if a subject is lost, they can always be found again. However, if a drivers license is lost, it is the same as if a subject is burned. The investigator will not be tailing that subject again.

If only one investigator is available for each
vehicle on a mobile tail, then each investigator should
have available a small, hand held cassette recorder which
can be operated with one hand. In this manner an investigator can dictate his notes into the cassette recorder while driving and have the notes transcribed onto
paper later. If an investigator has ever tried to drive
a vehicle, keep visual contact with a subject, and at the
same time attempt to write down notes, such as a plate
number off a vehicle, then he will appreciate the inven-
tion of the one hand operation cassette recorder.

As stated previously, the multiple vehicle tail is
conducted in essentially the same manner as a multiple
investigator foot tail. The first tail vehicle follows the
subject and the second tail vehicle lags behind the first.
The third tail vehicle parallels the subject from an
adjacent street. If the subject turns a corner, the
paralleling vehicle is contacted by radio, informing the
investigator of that vehicle of the subjects new direction.
The paralleling vehicle picks up the subject at that intersection and becomes the direct tail vehicle. The direct
tail vehicle continues through the intersection that the
subject turned at, to the next intersection, and then turns
in the same direction as the subject had. The direct tail
vehicle is now the new paralleling vehicle. The lag
vehicle approaches the intersection the subject turned at,
cautiously, ensuring that the subject did not turn the

corner and stop. If the subject had continued, the lag vehicle turns the same corner and picks up the tail as the lag vehicle for the new direct tail vehicle. During the course of the mobile tail, all vehicles can switch positions, called leap frogging, so that the same vehicle is not continuously behind the subject.

If a subject pulls over to a curb and stops, the direct tail vehicle should not stop immediately. The direct tail vehicle should continue past the subject and pull over further ahead of the subject. However, immediately upon realizing that a subject is about to pull over, the direct tail vehicle should inform the lag vehicle, by radio. The lag vehicle can then pull over before the subject does. In this manner, when the subject pulls out away from the curb, the lag vehicle can pull out behind it. At the same time, the lag vehicle should notify the direct tail vehicle by radio so that the direct tail vehicle can pull out as the lag vehicle passes. The lag vehicle then becomes the direct tail vehicle and the old direct tail vehicle becomes the new lag vehicle. Of course, while all of this is going on, the parallel vehicle is kept informed by radio.

STAKE-OUT

The last type of surveillance to be discussed is the fixed stake-out. This is whereby the investigator watches a subject from a stationary position such as a vehicle parked inconspicuously, or from a building or other fixed

34

location. The first word on any surveillance is <u>Patience</u>. It can become very tedious for any investigator to sit for hours watching a place or thing, but an investigator must never leave the stake-out position without being relieved, first, by another investigator.

The ideal vehicle for use on a stake-out is a surveillance van or truck. A van or truck can be equipped with such elaborate equipment as video cameras and taping equipment, complex radio and listening devices, as well as equipment for the investigators comfort such as a portable toilet. When a surveillance van or truck is used, it should be parked at the surveillance location previous to the stake-out. The investigator should then get out and leave, being picked up by an associate. Later, when the stake-out is initiated, the investigator should be driven to the van or truck and dropped off. In this manner, an investigator conducting the stake-out can be relieved without the van or truck having to be moved.

If on a stake-out, and an investigator is confronted by a person as to what the investigator is doing, an investigator should never tell the truth. A pretext as to why the investigator is there should have already been developed by the investigator previous to initiaing the stake-out. This, of course, would also be true when the stake-out is conducted from a fixed location such as a building.

Whenever renting a place, such as an apartment or motel, an investigator should never give the real reason for renting. People love to talk, and if someone in the building knows that your reason for being present is to conduct a surveillance, or that you are a private investigator, the news will probably travel faster than the investigator.

When conducting a surveillance from a building, an investigator should be extremely careful if he must approach a window in order to observe the subject. When it becomes necessary to approach a window to observe the subject, especially with binoculars or a camera, an investigator should ensure that he will not be silhouetted from behind with a light from within the room. At night, when possible, all lights should be kept off within the room.

During all phases of a stake-out, detailed notes should be kept of every movement made by the subject, and everything that is observed in the surveillance area. Plate numbers of all vehicles encountering the subject should also be recorded for possible use at a later time.

Whenever an investigator has to leave a stake-out position such as an apartment or a motel room, he should never leave any equipment behind unless he is being relieved by another investigator. This is especially true when conducting a stake-out from a motel. All equipment should be locked in a case and, if possible, put in the investigators trunk. The clean up ladies for most motels are very inquisitive and nosy. If they come in to clean up your room and find extensive surveillance equipment set up by the window, the word may get out before the investigator can.

Remember; the most important thing to take on any surveillance or fixed stake-out is Patience. Without patience, an investigator is merely wasting his time.

Chapter-5

CIVIL LITIGATION

Oftentimes an investigator will be hired by an attorney to perform an investigation involving a civil litigation case to determine if a case is worth further proceedings by the attorney, and if so, for trial preparation of the case. Such a case might involve an automobile accident, a personal injury (whereby a person might have tripped and sustained an injury), a product liability, etc.

For a case such as this, it is the investigators function to uncover some form of evidence which can prove that either the attorney's client is innocent of, or that some other party is guilty of, some form of negligence. An attorney will not always want an investigator to perform an entire investigation. At times, an attorney may only desire that certain aspects of the case be investigated. An investigator should always determine from the start, exactly what the attorney desires so that valuable time is not spent in areas of no significance. A large portion of an investigators time will be spent attempting to locate and/or contact witnesses and interviewing the same in an attempt to obtain a signed statement. (Note: Interviews and statements will be covered in depth in chapter 6).

When assigned such a case, an investigator should obtain as much data from the attorney as possible in regard to all persons involved. A blank form, such as the example "Civil Litigation Information Sheet" which follows this chapter, can be used to ensure that as much information as possible has been obtained. A consent form, such as the example which follows this chapter, should be signed by the attorneys client so that the investigator can use it to obtain copies of reports necessary to complete the investigation.

Before field work commences, all data should be checked and verified as to its accuracy. Times, dates, names, addresses, and phone numbers should be confirmed. Attempt to lay out a plan of action for each case so that each phase of the investigation is performed in the most logical, expedient, and cost effective manner. This can save many hours by eliminating duplication of work and travel. It is imperative that all cases be carried out in a careful and methodical manner, always being cognizant of attention to detail.

Once field work has begun, it is extremely important that notes be taken during all phases of the investigation. A blank "Original Case Notes" form, such as the one which follows this chapter, can be used to record such notes. These notes should include everything an investigator has done involving the case. They should also include observations made by the investigator.

AUTOMOBILE ACCIDENT INVESTIGATION

When investigating an automobile accident, one of the first objectives is to obtain a copy of the accident report from the police. Attempt to get the names and badge numbers of all the police officers who took part in the investigation and copies of any other investigating officers reports. Attempt to learn what the weather was on the day the accident occured.

An investigator should attempt to obtain statements from all witnesses listed on the police report. If a witness states that they did not see anything, a statement, called a "negative statement", should be obtained in order that they cannot come back at a later date and change their story. If a witness refuses to give a statement, a brief report should be prepared and placed in the file stating why no statement for that witness is present. Include in this report any information that might have been obtained during the conversation with the witness.

A canvass of the area of the accident should be conducted by the investigator, talking to all persons at private homes and businesses in an attempt to locate other possible witnesses or information concerning the accident.

Photographs of the accident scene and all vehicles involved in the accident should be taken (See chapter 8 for details on investigative photography).

Measurements of the accident scene should be taken and a diagram drawn. This diagram should show the width of the road, curb heights, types and widths of ditches and shoulders, road contours, the length and width of tire marks, debris, gouges, etc. Measurements should be made from permanent objects that are not likely to move, such as telephone poles, mile markers, etc. Ensure that the numbers of these objects are recorded on the diagram. Obstructions to the drivers view, such as the height of bushes, walls, fences, etc. should also be recorded on the diagram.

Many police officers who respond to automobile accidents make their own personal notes while at the accident scene in order to assist them later while writing an accident report. An investigator can often obtain valuable information from these notes. An investigator should make every effort to talk to each police officer. They will not always let an investigator read their notes, but will usually tell the investigator what information is contained in them.

An investigator should always check all the local papers to determine if any newspaper articles were printed about the automobile accident. Oftentimes there is valuable information to be obtained from them. Any clippings obtained should be kept in the file and then copies attached to the final report.

PUBLIC ACCIDENT INVESTIGATION

This type of investigation would include such accidents as a person falling down and sustaining an injury. The investigators job is usually to attempt to determine negligence on the part of someone who can be held liable for the client's injury. Whether it be an uneven walking surface, an unmarked curb or hole, or a defective stairway, it is the investigators task to find with whom the negligence lies.

An investigator should follow the investigation techniques as outlined under automobile investigation. Ensure that a diagram and photographs of the scene are completed. The techniques are the same once the basic are learned and practiced. Determining where the negligence lies, and with whom, is the main point to remember.

PRODUCT LIABILITY INVESTIGATION

For this type of investigation, the investigators main task is to prove that a product of some type was liable for, or caused, an accident which resulted in an injury. It should also be determined that the negligence for the accident lies with the producer and/or distributor of that product. As well as following the basics already discussed for civil litigation investigations, the investigator should attempt to determine, if indeed a product was defective or designed wrong, was the producer and/or the distributor of that product aware of the defect.

CIVIL LITIGATION
INFORMATION SHEET

DATE REC'D: _____ FILE NAME: _____

FILE NO.: _____ ATTORNEY: _____

Date of Accident: _____ Time: _____ Day: _____

Weather: _____ Location: _____

_____ Police Dept. Handling: _____

_____ Officer(s): _____

PLAINTIFF

Name: _____ Telephone No.: _____

D.O.B.: _____ Address: _____

Vehicle: Year: _____ Make: _____ Model: _____

Color: _____ Lic.No.: _____ State: _____

Damages: _____

Owner of Vehicle: _____

Occupation of Plaintiff: _____

Employer: _____ Address: _____

_____ Telephone No.: _____

Injuries: _____

Hospital: _____

Insurance Co.: _____

DEFENDANT NO.1

Name: _____ Telephone No.: _____

D.O.B.: _____ Address: _____

Vehicle: Year: _____ Make: _____ Model: _____

Color: _____ Lic.No.: _____ State: _____

Damages: _____

(1)

CIVIL LITIGATION INFORMATION SHEET (CONT.)- Defendant No.1

Owner of Vehicle: _____

Occupation of Defendant: _____

Employer: _____ Address: _____

_____ Telephone No.: _____

Injuries: _____

Hospital: _____

Insurance Co.: _____

DEFENDANT NO.2

Name: _____ Telephone No.: _____

D.O.B.: _____ Address: _____

Vehicle: Year: _____ Make: _____ Model: _____

Color: _____ Lic. No.: _____ State: _____

Damages: _____

Owner of Vehicle: _____

Occupation of Defendant: _____

Employer: _____ Telephone No.: _____

Injuries: _____

Hospital: _____

Insurance Co.: _____

WITNESS'S

Name: _____ Telephone No.: _____

Address: _____

Employer: _____ Telephone No.: _____

Address: _____

Name: _____ Telephone No.: _____

Address: _____

(2)

44

CIVIL LITIGATION INFORMATION SHEET (CONT.)- Witness's

Employer: _____ Telephone No.: _____

Address: _____

Name: _____ Telephone No.: _____

Address: _____

Employer: _____ Telephone No.: _____

Address: _____

Name : _____ Telephone No.: _____

Address: _____

Employer: _____ Telephone No.: _____

Address: _____

Name: _____ Telephone No.: _____

Address: _____

Employer: _____ Telephone No.: _____

Address: _____

Name: _____ Telephone No.: _____

Address: _____

Employer: _____ Telephone No.: _____

Address: _____

ADDITIONAL INFORMATION

_____

_____

_____

_____

_____

_____

(3)

CONSENT FORM

Date: _____

I, _____, hereby consent and authorize my attorneys _____, Or their agents, _____, to examine, inspect, or obtain photostatic copies of any and all medical and/or doctors reports or records, hospital reports or records, x-ray or other medical reports and/or records of any kind or nature, interview all doctors and/or other attendants and all employers and former employers regarding all matters relating to examination, diagnosis, care and treatment of myself, earnings and loss of earnings, police accident and/or traffic reports, Sheriff's, State Police, or Highway Patrol records or reports.

I am willing that a photostat of this authorization be accepted with the same authority as the original.

S/S _____

Address: _____

_____

Witness: _____

Witness: _____

ORIGINAL CASE NOTES

INVESTIGATOR: _____ CASE: _____

DATE	TIME	NOTES

Chapter - 6

INTERVIEWS AND STATEMENTS

Much of an investigators time is spent interviewing persons such as witnesses, suspects, etc. The investigator often is required to take a written statement from such persons which is known as a signed statement. The investigator taking the statement is known as the interviewer and the person being interviewed is known as the interviewee. It is important that an investigator become proficient in both interviewing and statement taking techniques.

INTERVIEWS

When an investigator interviews a person, he is doing more than merely asking questions. When interviewing, the investigator is attempting to extract information which will be helpful in the course of the investigation, or answer questions which the investigator needs the answers to in order to give direction to further action to be taken by the investigator. The investigator should attempt, by the use of correct questioning techniques, to have the interviewee draw a word picture upon answering questions. Questions must be asked in a manner which will cause the interviewee to tell a story in chronological order.

The investigator should not ask leading questions which could cause the interviewee to attempt to draw a conclusion, or guess at an answer that they may feel the investigator is looking for. Leading questions tend to confuse an interviewee, and should be avoided at all times during an interview.

An example of a leading question is "Was the truck you saw parked at the rear of the store black?" This type of question could cause an interviewee to answer "yes", because they may think this is the answer the investigator wants to hear, or they really don't remember what color the truck was and say "yes" so that they don't appear stupid. A correct line of questioning would be "What was the color of the truck you say you saw parked at the back of the store?" In this manner of questioning, you are making the interviewee do some thinking as to what they actually saw. If the interviewee does not remember the color of the truck, then that will be the interviewees answer. This type of open-ended questioning also allows an interviewee to tell their own story and not the story the investigator may want to hear.

STATEMENTS

When taking a written statement, there is information that should be included at the beginning of every statement in order to identify the interviewee. This information can also be used at a later date to locate a witness if the witness should skip town when needed. The beginning of the statement should include the interviewee's full name, address, phone number, age (Date of Birth), marital status, occupation, name and address of employer, salary (if possible) and the date, time, and place the statement is being taken. This should be followed by an acknowledgement that the statement is made of the interviewees own free will without threat or promise.

Following this, the statement should include all the information the interviewee can remember in regard to the incident being investigated. If the investigator is writing the statement for the interviewee, the investigator should attempt to make at least one mistake per page, intentionally. In this manner, when the interviewee reads the statement before signing, the mistakes can be corrected. Each mistake should be corrected by having the interviewee place a line through the mistake, write in the correct word over it, and then initial the correction. If and when the time came for the witness to go to court, they would never be able to say that they had not read the statement before signing it. By having the interviewee correct and initial the mistakes on the statement, they are obligated to admit to making the statement.

When the investigator has obtained all the information pertinent to the incident, the statement should conclude with a sentence such as the following: "The above statement consists of number of pages and is true and correct to the best of my knowledge." The interviewee should then sign the statement directly below this without skipping a line. The date should also be included by the interviewee directly below this. The statement should then be witnessed by someone other than the investigator.

If after the statement is written the interviewee refuses to sign the statement, the investigator should attempt to have the interviewee at least initial the statement to the fact that the contents of the statement are true.

There are several things that should always be remembered by an investigator when going out to take a statement. All statements should be made on either yellow lined legal paper or on regular statement paper. All statements should be written in longhand with ink (never pencil), and always have an extra supply of paper and pens on hand. An investigator should also always carry a set of credentials indentifying himself and employer, and plenty of business cards.

Following this chapter is an example statement from an automobile accident witness, and an interview guide for automobile accidents, which with a small amount of change, can be used for other types of interviews.

EXAMPLE STATEMENT

I am John Smith, age 29 (D.O.B. 4-23-53), and
reside at apartment #24, Hill Crest Apartments,
Rte. 9, Poughkeepsie, N.Y. 12601. My phone number
is 914-434-0012, and I am single. I am employed
by International Computers Inc., ~~Vilet~~ Violet J.S. Ave., Hyde
Park, N.Y., as a computer technician. I make the
following statement at my apartment on July 19,1982
at 6:00 P.M., of my own free will without threat or
promise.

On June 3, 1981, I was driving a 1974 red Chevy
Nova, N.Y. Reg.#0107-AKA, west on Union Street in
the west bound lane towards the intersection of
Market St. and Union Ave. The time was approx. 3:00
P.M. and I was traveling at approx. 25 M.P.H. The
weather was clear and the pavement was dry. I was
traveling behind a blue Ford pickup truck which was
traveling at approx. the same speed as myself, west
in the west bound lane. As the blue Ford pickup
truck entered the intersection of Market St. and
Union Ave., a tan Ford station wagon traveling south
on Market St., at what appeared to be a high rate of
speed, entered the intersection of Market St. and
Union Ave., without stopping at the stop sign for
south bound traffic on Market St., and struck the blue

S/S _John Smith_

Ford pickup truck in the right front fender, causing
the back of the truck to skid left and stop just past
the intersection on the west side. The tan station
wagon stopped immediately upon hitting the truck. I
stopped my car immediately and jumped out. I found
that both drivers were men and neither were injured
badly. The driver of the tan station wagon was
bleeding from the nose. The driver of the truck who
jumped out of his vehicle asked me to drive to a
phone and call the police and ambulance. I did so
and when I returned to the scene the police and ambulance were already present. The police were talking to the driver of the pickup truck who was already
seated in the police car, and the man from the tan
station wagon was already in the ambulance. I gave
my name and address and a verbal statement to the
police in regard to what I saw and then I left the
scene of the accident.

This is all I remember in regard to the accident
and the above statement consists of two (2) pages
and is true and correct to the best of my knowledge.

S/S _John Smith_

Date: _July 19, 1982_

Witness: S/S _Margret Smith_

Date: _7-19-82_

Witness: S/S _Bob Smith_

Date: _July 19-1982_

INTERVIEW GUIDE

IDENTITY OF PERSON

1. Full name.
2. Address. (Prior addresses.)
3. Telephone number. (Area code.)
4. Age. (Date of birth, if possible; With women use tact.)
5. Marital status. (Given name of spouse, number and ages of children.)
6. Occupation. (Exact duties.)
7. Name and address of employer. (Determine nature of business, if in doubt.)
8. Salary, commission.

CAR DRIVEN

1. Owner of car
2. Description of car. (Include registration number.)
3. Driver of car at time of accident.

EVENTS BEFORE ACCIDENT

1. Where was car coming from before the accident.
2. Purpose of the trip.
3. Occupants position in the car.
4. Had anybody in the car been drinking?

OTHER CARS INVOLVED (IF ANY)

1. Owner of car.
2. Description of car. (Include registration number.)
3. Driver of car at time of accident.
4. Occupants position in car.

ACCIDENT LOCATION

1. Date.
2. Time.
3. Exact Location.
4. Road description and markings.
5. Weather conditions. (Include visibility, lighting, if at night.)
6. Speed limits.
7. Traffic controls.

ACCIDENT CHAIN OF EVENTS

1. Speed before accident.
2. Position of other cars when first seen. (Include direction of travel, approx. speed, distance, signals given.)

ACCIDENT CHAIN OF EVENTS (CONT.)

3. Position of other cars when danger was first realized.
4. Evasive action taken to avoid accident. (If any.)
5. Position of cars at time of impact.
6. Points of impact.

DETAILS FOLLOWING THE ACCIDENT

1. Position of cars.
2. Course of cars and distance traveled after impact.
3. Skid marks. (Were they measured?)
4. Debris.
5. Conversation of any persons involved.
6. Police investigation.

DAMAGES

1. Extent.
2. Disposition of cars involved.
3. Estimates.

INJURIES

1. Extent.
2. Treatment. (Where and by whom.)
3. Previous disabilities. (Illness or injuries?)
4. Expected future disability.
5. Bills and loss of wages.

WITNESSES

1. Identity.
2. Location.
3. Relationships.
4. Did they actually see it?

Chapter – 7

UNDERCOVER INVESTIGATIONS

There are many misconceptions and preconceived images of the thrilling and exciting assignment as an undercover investigator, better known as an "undercover operative". However, the actual task of performing the functions of an undercover operative is anything but exciting. It is a very exacting and perservering job which demands a concentrated effort to accomplish two jobs at one time without neglecting either. An operative must fulfill the role which he or she is playing, without attracting suspicion, and simultaneously obtain information which he or she were placed undercover to procure.

SELECTION AND SCREENING

When screening applicants for the position of undercover operative, there are several areas that should be thoroughly examined.

One of the most important qualities that an undercover operative should possess is a good memory and the power to retain details and information without writing them down.

An undercover operative must be psychologically sound and have a gregarious personality. An undercover operative must be able to work alone without assistance, and yet not be an introvert. Never utilize an operative that shows an unfavorable uneasiness about an assignment.

All applicants should take a polygraph test to ensure

honesty. It has been revealed in the past that some undercover operatives have been just as dishonest, if not more so,
that the persons they were supposed to be catching. Honesty
in an operative is also important in order to ensure that an
over zealous operative does not resort to entrapment in order
to please his or her superiors. This type of action can only
lead to trouble down the road.

An investigation should be conducted on each applicant
to ensure that a history of overindulgence does not exist in
regard to drugs, alchol, or womanizing. The reason for this
is obvious.

PREPARATION FOR ASSIGNMENT

An operative should be chosen for an assignment who is
acquainted with the type of work involved. You would not
want to place an operative who is acquainted with construc-
tion undercover as a hair dresser.

Once a suitable operative for the assignment has been
selected, a briefing must be held. During this briefing the
operative is given his or her new identity. Attempt only to
change an operatives last name as he or she will readily respond to that name if called off guard. The operative should
receive documents such as identification cards to use to verify this new identity. A new background must be invented.
Try to stay as close to the operative's actual past as possible. Use cities and towns that the operative is familiar
with. If someone should question the operative about these
locations, the operative will be better able to answer. The

secret is to make the background simple yet believable. The operative should be closely worked with when making up this data. Then go over and over it until the operative can answer questions without hesitation.

If an operative is to work at a particular place of business, ensure that an employment application is on file there. If someone becomes suspicious and checks the files, the operative's cover will not be disclosed.

WORKING UNDERCOVER

The first thing that a client must understand is that no one is to know that an undercover operative is working for him or her. There are no exceptions, not even the clients wife!

An operative should dress according to the part being played. If an operative goes undercover as a laborer, he or she should dress as a laborer. He or she should not dress in a business suit. The operative should wear used clothes and if tools are involved, they should be used also. If any type of slang or special phraseology is connected with the job, the undercover operative should be familiar with it.

While undercover, an operative should never carry iden-tification that could reveal his or her true identity. An operative should always attempt to memorize as much infor-mation as possible. Never carry any information written down that would be suspicious or incriminating if found on your person.

If an operative has to meet with a client or employer, the meeting place should be set up in advance. A meeting should never be held at the same place twice. If phone contact must be made, it should always be done at a phone booth. Never take a chance using a regular phone as it may be bugged.

Remember, an undercover assignment is a painstaking and laborious task. It is not a job for every investigator. A operative must be screened, prepared for assignment, and then discreetly placed undercover. There are no short cuts and no tricks. It sometimes takes many months before the information desired is exposed.

Chapter – 8

INVESTIGATIVE PHOTOGRAPHY

This chapter does not propose to be a study in the technical functions or intricate components of photography or equipment. However, due to the fact that an investigator will inevitably become involved with photography in some manner during the course of his or her career, this chapter is presented as a general discussion. It will include sections on equipment, purpose of photography for investigations, and methods of investigative photography. In order to gain a better understanding of cameras and photography, a basic photography course would be of value to any investigator.

EQUIPMENT

An investigators assemblage of equipment is based on the extent of which the equipment will be used. All investigators should possess some type of an instant camera. This type of camera allows an investigator to see immediately if the photo will encompass everything which the investigator desires to appear in the photograph.

An investigator should also have access to a good 35MM single-lens reflex camera. This camera should have several lenses of bayonet type attachment, as opposed to screw type attachment, so that lenses can be changed quickly.

Several lenses should be available for different situations. For civil litigation, a 50MM lense is necessary. This lense reproduces scenes at their least amount of distortion so that the scene appears as close as it would to the naked eye. For surveillance cases, either several telephoto or mirror type lenses are necessary. Initially a 135MM and either 200MM or 300MM lense should suffice for most cases. However, if surveillance becomes your specialty, a 500MM lense or larger may be desirable. It must be understood that the larger the telephoto or mirror lense, the less movement the camera will tolerate without blurring the finished picture. A shoulder stock, which the camera and lense can be mounted on, is a good idea for lenses of 300MM and up. This will allow the investigator to steady the camera while photographing. For photo's, whereby concealment is not a necessity, a good tripod will also be an invaluable tool.

For cases whereby a automobile must be photographed, a flash unit will be desirable. A flash unit will be useful for fill-in light when photographing inside or underneath an automobile is necessary.

Film is also a very important consideration for the investigator. Film has a layer of emulsion which contains halide crystals which are sensitive to light. The size of these crystals determine the films light sensitivity, better known as the films speed. The smaller the crystals, the less sensitivity. The larger the crystals, the greater the sensitivity. The greater the sensitivity a film has, the less amount of light you require to produce a picture. The speeds available to a photographer are designated by ASA numbers. These numbers were established by the American Standards Association. Additionally, the size of the light sensitive crystals also determine the grain of a photograph. The grain of a photograph means the sharpness of the image. The larger the crystals, the grainier, or less sharp, the image will appear. This oftentimes means a trade-off for the investigator. A high film speed is often desirable for surveillance work because it is better for low light situations. However, the sharpness of the image is also important for identification purposes. This often necessitates the use of a slower film in order to obtain a sharper image. The investigator will have to experiment in order to know what film will give the best results for the job.

PURPOSE OF PHOTOGRAPHY

Photography is basically used during the course of an investigation to preserve details or circumstances of an event or situation to be used at a later date. Oftentimes, photographs will be used during the settlement or trial of a lawsuit or criminal proceeding.

Whenever an investigator shoots photographs, he or she should record certain information for each photograph. The date and time of each photo should be recorded as well as the weather conditions at the time the photo was taken. The subject being photographed, the distance and height from the subject should also be recorded. For each roll of film, an investigator should also record the file number, camera used, lense used, film used, and any remarks which might aid the investigator at a later date in explaining how the photo was taken. An example Photo Data sheet follows this chapter.

If a professional photographer is employed to take photographs for an investigator, it should be prearranged that not only the photos are desired, but the negatives as well. On some occasions, a free lance photographer will have been at the scene of an accident and will offer to sell the photos to an investigator. Every effort should be made by the investigator to buy the negatives as well as the photos. By possessing the negatives, it will deny other persons from obtaining the same photos. This can often be an ace in the hole for an investigator or attorney.

METHODS OF PHOTOGRAPHING

The cardinal rule for any investigator is that you can never take too many photographs. It is always the photo you fail to take that you will need at a later date.

During an investigation such as an accident, photograph all vehicles or persons involved. Include all four sides of an automobile, even if no damage exists on all sides. Take a photo of the the license plate as well,for identification purposes. Take photos of the inside, especially showing any damage such as a broken steering wheel or pushed in dashboard or floor. Take photos from as many angles as possible. Don't forget to look under the automobile. There may be damage caused by the accident, or a situation may exist which might have contributed to the accident.

Take as many photographs as possible at the scene of the accident. It may take a couple of years before the case goes to court and, by that time, the scene may have changed. Don't forget to photograph such possible evidence as skid marks, damage to property or trees, or pieces of the involved automobiles which might have remained at the scene.

For surveillance photography, the important points to remember are camera support, concealment, and lighting. An investigator should attempt to steady the camera by any means available. A tripod or shoulder stock are the preferred choices. However, for concealment purposes, a tree, fence, door jamb, or holding the camera against a wall may be the necessary choice. The occasion may arise whereby the camera may have to be concealed with a coat or newspaper on the investigators lap while seated. In a case such as this, the camera should be prefocused and preaimed. The investigator then has only to squeeze the shutter release when the subject enters the preaimed area.

Lighting is always an important factor to consider. Oftentimes a surveillance position will be set up during daylight hours. The camera is set for the proper exposure and the investigator waits for the target subject to appear. However, when the target subject finally appears, darkness has set in. The investigator should have taken the reduced light situation into account and reset the exposure before the subject appeared.

As with anything, an investigator must practice photo-graphic techniques if he or she hopes to be proficient. As stated at the beginning of this chapter; a good basic course in photography would be a great benefit to any investigator. There is no substitution for education.

PHOTO DATA

Photographer:		Date:		Time:	
Weather & Conditions:					
File Name:					
File No.:		Camera:			
Lense:		Film:		A.S.A.:	
Remarks:					

Photo No	SUBJECT	Distance From Subject	LOCATION	REMARKS
1				
2				
3				
4				
5				
6				
7				
8				
9				
10				
11				
12				
13				
14				
15				
16				
17				
18				
19				
20				

Chapter-9

REPORTS

A very important aspect of being an investigator is being able to explain in words what you did during the course of your investigation. It is not enough to only be proficient at obtaining information which is desired. An investigator must be a skilled and competent report writer.

When conducting an investigation, you know what you did and observed. You also took detailed notes so that you would not forget the details. However, you must now compile this data into a report so that your client will know what you did and observed.

There are certain things that should be included in all reports. The first is the agency's name and address. This is usually contained on the agency letterhead. Other data that should also be included at the beginning of a report are the date, case name and number, and the clients name and address. This information should be followed by the actual details of your findings.

When writing the details of the investigation, an investigator should attempt to include as many details as possible without including irrelevant information. The more details that are included in the report, the more an investigator has to work with should he have to make an appearance in court. Always include the who, what, when, where and how. Reports should always be written in chronological order according to events taking place. Only include information that is complete and relevant to the matter under investigation.

Each type of case should be presented in a different format. By having formats to use, reports are set up the same way each time a report is done. This allows for ease of reading by either clients or attorneys. Following this chapter, several formats are presented which can be utilized to organize information into final reports. Following these are blank formats which can be used for diagrams and mounting photographs as attachments to a report.

<u>OUTLINE FOR REPORT COVERSHEET</u>
(On Agency Letterhead)

Date

Name (of attorney or client)
Street Address
City, State, Zip Code

Attn: (Person receiving report)

RE: Name of file
    File No. (Their file No. if any).
    Our File No. (Your agency file No.).

Dear _____:

The attached report is the result of our handling

and investigation in accordance with your request

of _____.

This concludes our handling of this investigation

to date. I trust the facts and information are

satisfactory. If there are any questions or addi-

tional information desired, please feel free to

contact this office.

Professionally yours,

Your Name
Your Title (Chief Investigator, etc.)

Attachment(s)

ACCIDENT CASE REPORT OUTLINE

ACCIDENT DATE: Date, day of week and time.

LOCATION: Street (road or highway), city (town),
County and State.

PLAINTIFF: Identify completely to include full name,
address, phone number, place of employ-
ment, etc. In this paragraph give a synopsis of the plaintiff's signed statement
(if one has been obtained) or if interviewed only, give full details. Identify
plaintiff's vehicle and insurance carrier.

DEFENDANT: Handle the same as for plaintiff. (Note:
In some cases there will be more than one
defendant, in which case indicate as Defendant #1 (Operator), Defendant #2 (Owner)
and so forth.

WITNESSES: Identify completely as with the plaintiff,
giving a synopsis of any signed statement
if obtained and if not, complete details
of the results of the interview.

OTHER CONTACTS: Handle the same as the preceding. Include
a separate paragraph for each contact.

DESCRIPTION
OF SCENE: Describe the characteristics of the street
or highway, or other place, to include
type of pavement, lane markings, traffic
controls, obstacles and so forth.

ATTACHMENTS: List each item separately such as police
accident report, diagram of scene, signed
statements of individuals, photographs,
etc.

REMARKS: Enter any remarks which may tend to clarify or supplement information contained
in the report.

SURVEILLANCE REPORT OUTLINE

SUBJECT #1: (Primary subject) Identify completely to in-
            clude full name, address, phone number, de-
            scription in detail, place of employment if
            pertinent, etc. Include type(s) of vehicles
            driven, style, color, and registration number.

SUBJECT #2: Handle the same as for subject #1. (Note: in
            some cases there will be more than two subjects.
            List all involved subjects in the same manner
            as subject #1).

DATE:

TIME: Explain in detail exactly what was observed.

TIME:

TIME:

TIME:

TIME:

TIME:

DATE: (Start each new day after 12 midnight with a
            new date heading).

TIME:

TIME:

TIME:

TIME:

TIME:

TIME:

TIME:

ATTACHMENTS: List any attachments such as photographs.
             Describe each photograph explaining what it
             shows or represents.

REMARKS: Enter any remarks which may tend to clarify
             or supplement information contained in the
             report.

CRIMINAL CASE REPORT OUTLINE

DATE OF INCIDENT: Date, day of week and time.

LOCATION: Include exact location, i.e.: address, room, floor, alley, etc. Include city (town), County and State.

PLAINTIFF: Include State, County and court.

DEFENDANT: Identify completely to include name, address and/or facility being held at, phone number, etc. In this paragraph give a synopsis of the defendants interview, if any. If more than one defendant is involved, list as Defendant #1, Defendant #2, etc.

WITNESSES: LIST EACH ON A SEPARATE SHEET.* Identify completely to include full name, address, phone number, place of employment, etc. In this paragraph give a synopsis of interview or signed statement if obtained.

OTHER CONTACTS: LIST EACH ON A SEPARATE SHEET.* Handle the same as for witnesses.

ATTACHMENTS: List each item separately such as police reports, diagram of scene, signed statements, photographs, etc.

REMARKS: Enter any remarks which may tend to clarify or supplement information contained in the report.

* Each witness and contact should be listed on a separate sheet in the event that the testimony of that person is entered before the court as evidence. In this manner, only the testimony of that person will be seen by the other side. Otherwise, the testimony of another person, whose testimony might have been included on the same page, would also be seen by the other side. The testimony of that person may not be favorable to the side you are working for.

EXAMPLE BLANK DIAGRAM SHEET

ATTACHMENT NUMBER:

DATE SCENE MEASURED:

APPROX. SCALE:

ATTACHMENT NUMBER:	PHOTOGRAPH NUMBER:

PHOTOGRAPH MOUNTING FORM

(This portion would be utilized

for mounting a 5x7 photograph)

Chapter – 10

YOUR OWN AGENCY

There are one of two ways in which you may operate as a private investigator. First, you can work for a private investigation agency as an investigator for that firm; or you can start your own agency.

REQUIREMENTS

Each state has different requirements which must be fulfilled before a person can obtain a license to operate as a private investigator. Because each state is different, you must first determine who is responsible for the licensing of private investigators in your state. In some states, the Department of State issues licenses. Some states issue licenses at a county or local level. Check with your local law enforcement agency. They should know who the licensing agent is for your state.

Once you have determined who issues the license for your state, write for a list of requirements. Usually, a person must work as an apprentice investigator for a licensed agency for a predetermined amount of years before they qualify to apply for a license. Some states also allow ex-police officers, who functioned as an investigator for a predetermined amount of years, to qualify to apply for a license.

Once it can be proved that the experience qualification has been fulfilled, all or some of the following requirements must be satisfied before a license will be issued:

1) Extensive background and criminal investigation of applicant.

2) References as to your personal integrity from persons who have known you for a predetermined amount of years.

3) A written examination to determine, not only that you understand investigative technique, but that you understand your state laws governing private investigators. (A booklet is normally issued from the licensing agent of your state which explains your state rules and regulations governing private investigators.)

4) A license fee must be paid which must be re-submitted every time the license is renewed. Depending on your state, a license fee may be good for one to several years, before it must be renewed.

5) A surety bond, usually in the amount of $10,000.00, must be posted to correspond with the date the license is issued.

THE INVESTIGATORS OFFICE

An investigator should choose his or her office very carefully. An office can be rented, or an investigator can work from his or her private residence. The decision is up to the individual investigator.

However, there are pros and cons to each place which should be considered before making a decision. If an investigator rents an office, it can become very expensive. Sometimes, an investigator will work from his or her residence until they have a good following of clients, and then they make a transition to a rented office. On the other hand, if an investigator works from a private residence, he or she has only one rent or mortgage to pay.

With a rented office, an investigator can have clients come to the office for consultations. However, if an investigator is working from his or her residence, they may not desire clients coming to their house. Reasons may range from not wanting persons to know where they live for security reasons, to not wanting to be bothered at all times of the day or night.

If a private residence is utilized, a seperate area should be set aside as an office. Preferably, this area should have a seperate entrance so that clients do not have to travel through the investigator's house in order to get to the office.

A private investigator is a professional and his or her office should reflect that. The decor of an office should be tasteful, not tacky. A desk does not have to be cleared to look professional, but it should appear neat. No files should be in a position whereby one client could identify another client.

A private investigator should have some form of a 24 hour telephone answering service. Again, as a professional, an investigator should not have wives, children, or friends answer the phone. If they must, it should be prearranged that they answer with the agency name, followed by "May I help you". It is preferred that a 24 hour answering service is retained to answer the phone when the investigator is out of the office.

If an answering machine must be utilized, ensure that the out-going message is done in a professional manner. A preferred message would be "You have reached the ABC Investigation Agency. Unfortunately we are unable to answer our phone at this time. (For security reasons, never say nobody is there or you are out of town.) If you will leave your name, date, and time of call, and a brief message, I will return your call as soon as possible". Never leave a message such as "This is Joe Doe, I'm not in now, leave a message and I'll get back with you". Again, always present yourself as a professional.

OFFICE EQUIPMENT

There are several pieces of equipment that are essential for every private investigator's office. They are: 1)a desk, 2) a filing cabinet, and 3) a typewriter. All three of these items should be of the best quality affordable as they will be utilized the most of all the equipment in the office.

File cabinets should be of the full suspension type so that they can support of weight of large files. Hanging file folders should be used in the file cabinet as they can accomo-date larger files, will maintain files in a neat and orderly fashion, and prevent files from sliding down and under other files. Files may be filed by either case name alphabetically or by file number. All cases should be assigned a case number. A case log sheet should be utilized to record file names and numbers so they can be maintained in an orderly manner. An example of a case log sheet follows this chapter. The date the case was received and the date the case was closed can also be recorded on this sheet. Upon completion of a case, 3" x 5" file cards should also be maintained in order to recall file names and individuals that were involved in each case. An example of both a Case Name file card and an Individual Name file card follow this chapter.

The name of the investigation agency should be printed on all stationery and envelopes. A rubber stamp may be used initially, but printed matter should be purchased as soon as affordable as it has a more professional appearance and it tends to give the impression that the agency is solvent and not just a fly-by-night operation. Business cards are also a must. They should include the agency name, address, telephone number, and the owner's name.

As the agency grows other equipment such as a dictation machine, transcription machine, copy machine, etc. will become necessary in order to speed the office process. However, this type of equipment is a very expensive proposition and should only be purchased on an as needed basis.

HANDLING OF CLIENTS

When a potential client comes to you, he or she normally has a problem that they are hoping you can solve. If they are angry, upset, or depressed, your first task is to comfort them. However, always remain professional. Don't get involved with taking sides in hopes a potential client will hire you because you sided with them. Your advice must be sound and professional.

It is imperative that you determine at the onset of the initial consultation the approximate cost for the type of investigation the potential client desires. Ensure that the potential client understands the approximate cost and your pricing structure, i.e.: hourly rate, mileage rate, and all expenses incurred. Be certain that the potential client can afford these prices. If they can't afford you, explain that you are very sorry, but you don't believe you can help them. Don't negotiate on price. It will only cheapen your image. Have a set price and stand by it. A very prestigious case or client will be of no value if you are not paid for your services. You are a professional and should be paid as such. Leave non-profit work to non-profit organizations.

Once you decide to accept a case, the first thing you should do is get a signed contract between your agency and the client. This type of contract is called an "Agreement For Service". This agreement should contain the date, client's name, address, and telephone number. It should specifically state the type of services being retained, i.e.: surveillance, civil litigation, internal theft, etc. Also include the location of services. The agreement should state that they are subscribing to your services, at the rate you charge per hour, plus expenses and mileage at the rate you charge per mile. State that you will notify the client when the cost of services, including expenses and mileage, has reached a dollar amount agreed upon by both you and the client. State the period of time the agreement shall cover and a minimum period it shall remain in force. It should also be stated that the client shall notify you in writing if additional services are authorized. The retainer amount that you require upon signing the agreement should be recorded as well as the fact that the balance shall be paid in full prior to the release of any information developed. Ensure that the client understands that the fee is not contigent upon, or related to, the services performed or charged by others, or information and details developed. The client should also understand that all information developed and submitted to the client shall be treated as strictly confidential and shoud not be released to anyone without written authorization from you. Any "Agreement For Service" that you draw up for use by your agency should be checked by your attorney for legal content before you use it. (An example "Agreement For Service" follows this chapter.)

When the agreement is signed, you should then set up a file for your new case. Assign the case a file number and fill out a case work sheet (see example following this chapter). The case work sheet should contain the file number, file name, client's name, and client's attorney or firm name, if any. The case work sheet will be used as the investigation progresses to keep track of the hours, mileage, and expenses. In this manner, when the case is completed, it is a simple matter to determine the total cost of services.

A FINAL WORD

You are the investigator! Don't allow clients to run your investigations. You should conduct all investigations as you see fit. If a client wishes to assist or direct, inform them that you must insist that they remain detached from the actual investigation. They have hired you to conduct the investigation and they must allow you to do your job. The only exception should be when the client is an attorney. An attorney may only desire certain aspects of an incident investigated, or certain persons interviewed. Under these circumstances, it is the attorney's case and he or she knows what they want.

The career of a private investigator can be exciting and prosperous. Never lose site of the fact that you are in business to help people who have problems. Always be fair with your clients and NEVER compromise your position as a professional or the honerable profession of private investigation.

CASE LOG

DATE REC'D	FILE NUMBER	NAME OF CASE	DATE - CLOSED

FILE CARDS

CASE NAME FILE

CASE NAME:

CASE NUMBER:

TYPE:

CLIENT:

PLAINTIFF:

DEFENDANT:

INDIVIDUAL NAME FILE

NAME (last, first, middle):

CASE NUMBER:

CASE NAME:

TYPE:

CONNECTION: (I.E., plaintiff, defendant, witness, etc.)

AGREEMENT FOR SERVICE

CLIENT: _____ DATE: _____

ADDRESS: _____ CASE NO.: _____

CITY: _____ TELEPHONE: _____

TYPE OF SERVICE: _____

LOCATION OF SERVICE: _____

The undersigned hereby subscribes to the services of _(Name of your firm)_ as set forth in this agreement. This shall consist of _(Number of investigators)_ performing services as shown above at the rate of $_____ per hour, plus expenses and mileage at the rate of $_____ per mile. Cost of services shall not exceed $_____ per 8 hour period, exclusive of expenses and mileage. _(Name of your firm_ shall notify the client when cost of services, including expenses and mileage, has reached $_____. This agreement shall cover a period of _____ and remain in force for a minimum period of _____. The client will then notify _(Name of your firm)_ in writing if additional services are authorized.

Upon signing of this agreement, a retainer of $_____ has been paid, the balance of cost for services will be paid upon a statement of services being received and prior to the release of any information developed. The balance shall be paid in full and the fee for services shall be paid directly to _(Name of your firm_. This fee is not contingent upon or related to services performed or charged by others, or information and details developed.

If services are cancelled or stopped by the client, the retainer shall be forfeited and any services, expense, mileage or other cost which exceed the amount of the retainer shall be paid in full upon receipt of a statement of services and prior to any information developed being released. This agreement shall be terminated immediately upon receipt of written notice by either party.

ALL INFORMATION DEVELOPED AND SUBMITTED TO CLIENT OR HIS OR HER AUTHORIZED REPRESENTATIVE SHALL BE TREATED AS STRICTLY CONFIDENTIAL AND NOT RELEASED TO ANYONE ELSE WITHOUT WRITTEN AUTHORIZATION. CONDITIONS NOT PRINTED OR WRITTEN ABOVE ON THIS AGREEMENT ARE NOT BINDING ON EITHER PARTY.

_____ DATE: _____
            Client

_____ DATE: _____
      (Name of your firm)

CASE WORK SHEET

FILE NO.: _____ FILE NAME: _____

CLIENT: _____ ATTORNEY/FIRM: _____

| DATE | AGENT | HOURS | | | | EXPLAIN | MILES | TEL. | PHOTS | REP'Ts | MISC. | EXPLAIN |
		OFFICE	INVEST.	SURV.	MISC.							

TELEPHONE: .... $ _____ OFFICE: _____ hrs. @ $ _____ per. hr. = $ _____ HRS. $ _____

PHOTOGRAPHS: ..... $ _____ INVESTIGATION: _____ hrs. @ $ _____ per. hr. = $ _____ MIL. $ _____

REPORTS: .... $ _____ SURVEILLANCE: _____ hrs. @ $ _____ per. hr. = $ _____ EXP. $ _____

MISC.: .... $ _____ MISC.: _____ hrs. @ $ _____ per. hr. = $ _____ SUBTL. $ _____

TOTAL EXPENSES: $ _____ TOTAL HOURS: _____ -RET. $ _____

RETAINER: $ _____ MILEAGE: _____ miles @ _____ per mile = $ _____ TOTAL $ _____

SOURCES OF INFORMATION

1. CITY ASSESSOR

   The city Assessor's office has available maps of all the property within that city. They also have a list of the owners for that property and its assessed value.

2. CITY DIRECTORIES

   City directories can normally be obtained for most cities within a state. They will normally be cross referenced by street names and persons names. They will usually tell the name of the person or persons residing at that address, their telephone number and occupation. The major publisher of city directories is R.L. Polk & Co., 15 Riverview Business Park, 300 Commercial Street, Malden, Massachusetts, 02148.

3. COUNTY ASSESSOR

   The County Assessor's office has available the same information as the the City Assessor, except the information is maintained for the county. The County Assessor may also have aerial photographs of the county.

4. COUNTY CLERK

   The County Clerk maintains marriage license applications, civil files, probate records for estates, civil action, and criminal action indexes, and criminal files.

5. COUNTY RECORDER

   The County Recorder (County records section) is a wealth of information. The County Recorder maintains records of all DBA (Doing Business As) certificates which list all registered business of that county alphabetically by business name. It will include the business address, owner and owner's address. The same records are maintained on corporations in the county. Also, records are maintained on all real estate transactions including information on deeds and mortgages, powers of attorney, judgements against real property, military service discharges, pistol permits issued, death, birth, marriage and coroner's certificates.

6. CREDIT BUREAUS

   Most local businesses belong to a credit bureau. A business owner who subscribes to the services of such a bureau (And who just happens to be the same business owner that you have developed a friendly relationship with) can usually run a

credit check on a person for you. A credit check will
reveal such information a the person's employment history, address (and past addresses), social security number and payment habits.

7. CROSS REFERENCE DIRECTORIES

Cross Reference or Reverse Directories list telephone
numbers in numerical order and street addresses in alpha-
betical order. They list the person to whom the telephone
number or address belongs. A good source for a cross reference directory is Hill-Donnelly, 2602 South MacDill
Avenue, P.O. Box 14417, Tampa, Florida 33690.

8. DEPARTMENT OF MOTOR VEHICLES

The Department of Motor Vehicles for each state can supply
several types of information. First, if you have a license
plate number, they can tell you the owner of that vehicle.
their date of birth, address, insurance company (by code
number), date of expiration for that registration, vehicle
year, make, type and color. Second, if you have a person's
name and date of birth (an address helps, but is not necessary) they can tell you what vehicle are registered to that
person along with the information listed in the first section. Third, an abstract can be obtained on each licensed
driver which will reveal what violations that driver has
had, whether their license has ever been suspended or re-
voked, etc. The following is a list of where to write in
each state for DMV information:

ALABAMA

Driver License Division
Certification Section
P.O. Box 1471
Montgomery, Alabama 36102

ALASKA

Department of Public Safety
Drivers License Section
Juneau, Alaska 99801

ARIZONA

Motor Vehicle Division
1739 W. Jakson Street
Phoenix, Arizona 85007

ARKANSAS

Drivers Licensing Section
P.O. Box 1272
Little Rock, Arkansas 72203

CALIFORNIA

Department of Motor Vehicles
Division of Drivers Licenses
P.O. Box 1231
Sacramento, California   95812

COLORADO

Colorado Department of Revenue
Motor Vehicles Division
1375 Sherman Street
Dencer, Colorado   80203

CONNECTICUT

Department of Motor Vehicles
Copy Record Section
60 State Street
Wethersfield, Connecticut   06109

DELAWARE

Motor Vehicle Department
P.O. Box 698
Driver's License Section
Dover, Delaware   19901

DISTRICT OF COLUMBIA

Department of Motor Vehicles
Records Service
301 C Street N.W.
Washington, D.C.

FLORIDA

Drivers License Division
Department of Motor Vehicles
Neil Kirkman Building
Tallahassee, Florida   32304

GEORGIA

Department of Public Safety
Drivers Services Section
P.O. Box 1456
Atlanta, Georgia   30301

HAWAII

State of Hawaii
Violations Buteau
842 Bethel Street
Honolulu, Hawaii   96813

IDAHO

Department of Law Enforcement
Motor Vehicle Division
P.O. Box 34
Boise, Idaho 83731

ILLINOIS

Secretary of State
Drivers License Division
Centennial Building
Springfield, Illinois 62723

INDIANA

Bureau of Motor Vehicles
Division of Driver Licensing
Room 315, State Office Building
Indianapolis, Indiana 46209

IOWA

Department of Transportation
Records Section
State Office Building
Des Moines, Iowa 50319

KANSAS

Motor Vehicle Department
Driver's License Division
State Office Building
Topeka, Kansas 66612

KENTUCKY

Division of Driver Licensing
New State Office Building
Frankfort, Kentucky 40601

LOUISIANA

Department of Public Safety
Driver's License Division
P.O. Box 1271
Baton Rouge, Louisiana 70821

MAINE

Motor Vehicle Department
Bureau of Driver Improvement
and Financial Responsibility
242 State Street
Augusta, Maine 04333

MARYLAND

Motor Vehicle Administration
Driver Records Section
6601 Ritchie Highway, N.E.
Glen Burnie, Maryland 21601

MASSACHUSETTS

Registry of Motor Vehicles
100 Nashua Street
Boston, Massachusetts 02114

MICHIGAN

Michigan Department of State
Bureau of Driver and Vehicle Services
Lansing, Michigan 48918

MINNESOTA

Minnesota Department of Public Safety
Driver's License Office
State Highway Building
Saint Paul, Minnesota 55155

MISSISSIPPI

Mississippi Highway Safety Patrol
Drivers License Issuance Bureau
P.O. Box 958
Jackson, Mississippi 39205

MISSOURI

Bureau of Driver's License
P.O. Box 200
Jefferson City, Missouri 65101

MONTANA

Montana Highway Patrol
1014 National
Helena, Montana 59601

NEBRASKA

Department of Motor Vehicles
Driver License Division
P.O. Box 94789
Lincoln, Nebraska 68509

NEVADA

Department of Motor Vehicles
Drivers License Division
555 Wright Way
Carson City, Nevada   89701

NEW HAMPSHIRE

Commissioner of Motor Vehicles
State House
Concord, New Hampshire   03301

NEW JERSEY

Division of Motor Vehicles
Driver Absract Unit
25 South Montgomery Street
Trenton, N.J.   08666

NEW MEXICO

Department of Motor Vehicles
Bataan Memorial Building
Santa Fe, New Mexico   87501

NEW YORK

Department of Motor Vehicles
Empire State Plaza
Albany, New York   12228

NORTH CAROLINA

Department of Transportation
Driver License Division
Raleigh, North Carolina

NORTH DAKOTA

Safety Responsibility Division
State Highway Department
State Capital
Bismarck, North Dakota   58501

OHIO

Bureau of Motor Vehicles
P.O. Box 1199
Columbus, Ohio   43216

OKLAHOMA

Driver Records Service
Department of Public Safety
P.O. Box 11415
Oklahoma City, Oklahoma   73111

OREGON

Motor Vehicle Division
1905 Lana Ave.
Salem, Oregon 97301

PENNSYLVANIA

Pennsylvania Department of Transportation
Operator Information Section
Room 212
Transportation and Safety Building
Harrisburg, Pennsylvania   17120

RHODE ISLAND

Registry of Motor Vehicles
Room 101
State Office Building
Providence, Rhode Island   02903

SOUTH CAROLINA

South Carolina State Highway Department
Driver Record Check Station
Columbia, South Carolina   29202

SOUTH DAKOTA

Secretary of State
Motor Vehicle Director
Pierre, South Dakota   57501

TENNESSEE

Department of Safety
Andrew Jackson Building
Nashville, Tennessee   37219

TEXAS

Texas Department of Public Safety
License Issuance and Driver Records
P.O. Box 4087
Austin, Texas 78773

UTAH

Driver's License Division
314 State Office Building
Salt Lake City, Utah 84114

VERMONT

Motor Vehicle Department
Records Section
Montpelier, Vermont 05602

VIRGINIA

Division of Motor Vehicles
Driver Information
P.O. Box 27412
Richmond, Virginia 23269

WASHINGTON

Division of Driver Licensing
Department of Motor Vehicles
Olympia, Washington 98501

WEST VIRGINIA

Driver Improvement Division
Department of Motor Vehicles
1800 Washington Street East
Charleston, West Virginia 25305

WISCONSIN

Motor Vehicle Department
Hill Farms State Office Building
4802 Sheboygan Avenue
Madison, Wisconsin 53702

WYOMING

Wyoming Department of Revenue
Motor Vehicle Division
2200 Carey Avenue
Cheyenne, Wyoming 82001

9. NEWSPAPER FILES

Most newspapers have an article morgue where articles from
that newspaper are kept on file. These articles are normally cross referenced by subject, title and person involved.
Engagement announcements, wedding announcements, promotion
announcements, etc. are a great source for pictures.

10. POST OFFICE

By talking to the postal carrier who delivers to a particular location, you can usually obtain invaluable information in regard to the persons living at that residence.
A carrier, because he or she usually goes to the same residence's every day, five or six days a week, usually
knows when a person or family is on vacation, how many
people are in the family, how often they take their mail
out of their mail box, non-family members who may be living
there, descriptions of the residents, and the list goes on
and on. Also, if someone moves and leaves a change of address card at their post office, a postal clerk can supply
you with the new address for the fee of $1.00.

11. REGISTRAR OF VOTERS

If a person votes, they have their name registered at the
Registrar of Voters for their voting district. Their Registration card will reveal their name, address, place of
birth, occupation, signature, and registration date.

12. SCHOOLS

Schools have records of a students name, date of birth, address (and change of addresses), parents names, academic
standing, etc. Also, most school libraries have a collection
of past and current yearbooks which are another source for
photographs.

13. SOCIAL SECURITY NUMBERS

Social Security Numbers can reveal a great deal about anybody who has ever collected a paycheck. However, the Social
Security Administration will not release any information to
anyone (not even the police) in regard to the holder of a
social security number. But this does not mean that a social
security number is of no assistance to the investigator. The
first three numbers of a sicial security number are known as
the "area number" and indicates the state in which the initial application for the card was filed. This can be a great
help for charge application fraud control, employment application verification, identity verification, etc. The following is a list of the three digit codes with their corresponding state:

001 to 003   New Hampshire
004 to 007   Maine
008 to 009   Vermont
010 to 034   Massachusetts
035 to 039   Rhode Island
040 to 049   Connecticut
050 to 134   New York
135 to 158   New Jersey
159 to 211   Pennsylvania

```
212 to 220   Maryland
221 to 222   Delaware
223 to 231   Virginia
232 to 236   West Virginia
237 to 246   North Carolina (also 232)
247 to 251   South Carolina
252 to 260   Georgia
261 to 267   Florida
268 to 302   Ohio
303 to 317   Indiana
318 to 361   Illinois
362 to 386   Michigan
387 to 399   Wisconsin
400 to 407   Kentucky
408 to 415   Tennessee
416 to 424   Alabama
425 to 428   Mississippi (also 587)
429 to 432   Arkansas
433 to 439   Louisiana
440 to 448   Oklahoma
449 to 467   Texas
468 to 477   Minnesota
478 to 485   Iowa
486 to 500   Missouri
501 to 502   North Dakota
503 to 504   South Dakota
505 to 508   Nebraska
509 to 515   Kanasa
516 to 517   Montana
518 to 519   Idaho
520          Wyoming
521 to 524   Colorado
525 &  585   New Mexico
526 to 527   Arizona
528 to 529   Utah
530          Nevada
531 to 539   Washington
540 to 544   Oregon
545 to 573   California
574          Alaska
575 to 576   Hawaii
577 to 579   District of Columbia
580          Virgin Islands
581 to 585   Puerto Rico
586          Guam, American Samoa, Phillippine Islands
```

14. STATE HIGHWAY DEPARTMENT

The State Highway Department for each state has blueprints, diagrams, dimensions, sketch's, etc. for every state owned highway for that state. Copies can normally be obtained for a reasonable fee. These can be of great help on an automobile accident investigation (however if the state is a party to the suit, use a pretext for wanting the diagrams, etc.). County Highway Departments, Town and City Highway

Departments, etc. have the same available for their respective roads and streets.

15. STATE RECORDS

Copies of most records from each county, city, town, etc. go to the State. The State also maintains additional records. The Secretary of State (or its corresponding title for that state) maintain the licensing records which usually include private investigator's licenses, security guard agency licenses, realtor licenses, beautician licenses, or any other type of licenses which are issued by the State. The State also usually has a listing of the corporations of that state.

16. TELEPHONE DIRECTORIES

Telephone Directories are a good source to use to verify past addresses. By going back a year at a time, any change of address made by a person will be reflected in a phone book as long as that person maintained a listed phone number. This can really come in handy to verify past addresses on an employment application, etc. Libraries usually maintain phone books for years for their locality.

17. WHO'S WHO DIRECTORIES

There are many types of Who's Who Directories around. The original was Who's Who in America which contained data on prominent persons in America. However, now there are available who's who directories for prominent persons in the east, west, business, arts, politics, etc. Data is normally submitted by the persons included so it is your job to separate accuracy from egomania.

18. MARRIAGE RECORDS

An official record of every marriage should be available in the place where the event occured. These records may be filed permanently either in a State vital statistics office or in a city, county, or other local office. When writing for a copy, it is suggested that a money order or certified check be enclosed since the office cannot refund cash lost in transit. The following information will assist in locating the information you request:

1. Full names of bride and groom.
2. Residence address at time of marriage.
3. Age at time of marriage (or date of birth).
4. Date and place of marriage.
5. Purpose for which copy is needed.
6. Relationship to person whose record is on file.

A copy may be obtained by writing to the appropriate office listed below. Fees listed are subject to change.

ALABAMA

Records since August 1936: Bureau of Vital Statistics, State Department of Public Health, Montgomery, Alabama, 36104. Fee includes search and report, or copy of record if found. Cost $2.00.

Probate Judge in county where license was issued. Cost $1.00.

ALASKA

Records since 1913: Bureau of Vital Statistics, Department of Health and Welfare, Pouch H, Juneau, Alaska 99801. Cost $2.00.

AMERICAN SAMOA

Registrar of Vital Statistics, Pago Pago, American Samoa, 96920. Cost $1.00.

ARIZONA

Clerk of Superior Court in county where license was issued. Cost varies.

ARKANSAS

Records since 1917: Bureau of Vital Statistics, State Department of Health, Little Rock, Arkansas 72201. Cost $2.00.

County Clerk in county where license was issued. Cost $2.00.

CALIFORNIA

Bureau of Vital Statistics, State Department of Public Health, 744 P Street, Sacramento, California 95814. Cost $2.00.

CANAL ZONE

Balboa Division (Pacific Area), Clerk, U.S. District Court, Box 2006, Balboa Heights, Canal Zone. Cost $1.00.

Cristobal Division (Atlantic Area), Clerk, U.S. District Court, Box 1175, Cristobal, Canal Zone. Cost $1.00

COLORADO

Statewide index of records for all years except 1940-1967: Records and Statistics Section, Colorado Department of Health, 4210 East 11th Avenue, Denver, Colorado 80220. In-

COLORADO CONT.

quiries will be forwarded to appropriate county office.
Cost varies.

County Clerk in county where license was issued. Cost
varies.

CONNECTICUT

Records since July 1. 1897: Public Health Statistics Section, State Department of Health, 79 Elm Street, Hartford,
Connecticut 06115. Cost $1.00.

Registrar of Vital Statistics in town where license was
issued. Cost $1.00.

DELAWARE

Bureau of Vital Statistics, Division of Physical Health,
Department of Health and Social Services, State Health
Building, Dover, Delaware 19901. Cost $2.50.

DISTRICT OF COLUMBIA

Clerk, District of Columbia Court of General Sessions,
Washington, D.C. 20001. Cost $2.00 (Fee includes $1.00
for proof of marriage and $1.00 for application giving age
at time of marriage).

FLORIDA

Records since June 6, 1927: Bureau of Vital Statistics,
State Division of Health, P.O. Box 210, Jacksonville, Florida 32201. If year is unknown, the fee is $2.00 for the
first year searched and $1.00 for each additional year up
to a maximum of $25.00. Otherwise cost is $2.00. Fee includes a copy of the record if found.

County Judge in county where license was issued. Cost
varies.

GEORGIA

Records since June 9, 1952: Vital Records Service, Stae Department of Public Health, 47 Trinity Avenue, S.W. Atlanta,
Georgia 30334. All inquires will be forwarded to appropriate office and may be verified. Certified copies not available form State Health Department.

County Ordinary in county where license was issued. Cost
$2.00.

GUAM

Office of Vital and Health Statistics, Department of Public Health and Social Services, Government of Guam, P.O. Box 2816, Agana, Guam, M.I. 96910. Cost $1.00.

HAWAII

Research and Statistics Office, State Department of Health, P.O. Box 3378, Honolulu, Hawaii 96801. Cost $2.00.

IDAHO

Records since 1947: Bureau of Vital Statistics, State Department of Health, Boise, Idaho 83701. Cost $2.00.

County Recorder in county where license was issued. Cost varies.

ILLINOIS

Records since January 1, 1962: Bureau of Statistics, State Department of Public Health, Springfield, Illinois 62706. All items may be varified for a fee of $2.00 but certified copies are not available from the State health department.

County Clerk in county where license was issued. Cost $2.00.

INDIANA

Records since 1958: Division of Vital Records, State Board of Health, 1330 West Michigan Street, Indianapolis, Indiana 46206. Inquiries will be forwarded to the apppropriate office. Certified copies are not available from the State health department.

Clerk of Circuit Court, or Clerk of Superior Court, in county where license was issued. Cost varies.

IOWA

Division of Records and Statistics, State Department of Health, Des Moines, Iowa 50319. Cost $2.00.

KANSAS

Records since May 1913: Division of Vital Statistics, State Department of Health, Topeka, Kansas 66612. Cost $2.00.

Probate Judge in county where license was issued. Cost varies.

KENTUCKY

Records since July 1, 1958: Office of Vital Statistics,
State Department of Health, 275 East Main Street, Frankfort, Kentucky 40601. Cost $2.00.

Clerk of County Court in county where license was issued.
Cost varies.

LOUISIANA (Except New Orleans)

Records since 1946: Division of Public Health Statistics,
State Department of Health, P.O. Box 60630, New Orleans,
Louisiana 70160. Inquiries will be forwarded to appropriate office. Certified copies are not available from State
health department.

Clerk of Court in parish where license was issued. Cost
$2.00.

New Orleans

Bureau of Vital Statistics, City Health Department, 1W03
City Hall, Civic Center, New Orleans, Louisiana 70112.
Cost $2.00.

MAINE

Office of Vital Statistics, State Department of Health and
Welfare, State House, Augusta, Maine 04330. Cost $1.00.

MARYLAND

Records since June 1, 1951: Division of Vital Records,
State Department of Health and Mental Hygiene, State Office
Building, 301 West Preston Street, Baltimore, Maryland
21201. Additional copies of same record obtained at the
same time are $1.00. First copy $2.00.

Clerk of Circuit Court in county where license was issued
or Clerk of Court of Common Pleas of Baltimore. Cost varies.

MASSACHUSETTS

Records since 1841: Registrar of Vital Statistics, 272
State House, Boston, Massachusetts 02133. Earliest Boston
records are for the year 1848. Cost $1.00.

MICHIGAN

Records since April 1867: Vital Records Section, Michigan
Department of Health, 3500 North Logan Street, Lansing,
Michigan 48914. Cost $2.00.

County Clerk in county where license was issued. Cost varies.

MINNESOTA

Statewide index since January 1958: Section of Vital Statistics, State Department of Health, 717 Delaware Street, S.E., Minneapolis, Minnesota 55440. Inquires will be forwarded to appropriate office. Certified copies are not available from State Health Department.

Clerk of District Court in county where license was issued. Cost $2.00.

MISSISSIPPI

Records since January 1926: Vital Records Registration Unit, State Board of Health, P.O. Box 1700, Jackson, Mississippi 39205. Cost $2.00.

Circuit Clerk in county where license was issued. Cost $2.00.

MISSOURI

Records since 1948: Vital Records, Division of Health, State Department of Public Health and Welfare, Jefferson City, Missouri 65102. Free of charge.

Recorder of Deeds in county where license was issued. Cost varies.

MONTANA

Records since July 1943: Division of Records and Statistics, State Department of Health, Helena, Montana 59601. Inquiries will be forwarded to the appropriate office. No certified copies available from State health Department.

Clerk of District Court in county where license was issued. Cost varies.

NEBRASKA

Records since January 1909: Bureau of Vital Statistics, State Department of Health, State Capital, Lincoln, Nebraska 68509. Cost $2.00.

County Court in county where license was issued. Cost varies.

NEVADA

County Recorder in county where license was issued. Cost varies.

NEW HAMPSHIRE

Records since 1640: Department of Health and Welfare, Division of Public Health, Bureau of Vital Statistics, 61 South Spring Street, Concord, New Hampshire 03301. Cost $1.00.

Town Clerk in town where license was issued. Cost $1.00.

NEW JERSEY

State Registrar, State Department of Health, P.O. Box 1540, Trenton, New Jersey 08625. If year is unknown, the fee is an additional $0.50 for each calendar year to be searched. Cost $2.00.

For records from May, 1848 thru May 1878 write to the Archives and History Bureau, State Library Division, State Department of Education, Trenton, New Jersey 08625. No fee.

NEW MEXICO

County Clerk in county where marriage was performed. Cost varies.

NEW YORK (Except N.Y. City)

Records from January 1880 to December 1907 and since May 1915: Bureau of Vital Records, State Department of Health, Albany, New York 12208. Cost $2.00.

Records from January 1880 to December 1907: Write to City Clerk in Albany or Buffalo and Registrar of Vital Statistics in Yonkers, if marriage occured in these cities. Cost $2.00.

Records from January 1908 to April 1915: County Clerk in county where license was issued. Cost varies.

New York City

Records from 1847 to 1865: Municipal Archives and Records Retention Center, New York Public Library, 23 Park Row, New York, New York 10038, except Brooklyn records for this period, which are filed with County Clerks Office, Kings County, Supreme Court Building, Brooklyn, New York 11201. Cost $3.06.

Records from 1866 to 1907: City Clerk's Office in Borough in which marriage was performed. Cost $3.06.

Records from 1908 to May 12, 1943: Residents-City Clerk's Office in borough of bride's residence; non-residents-City Clerk's Office in borough in which license was obtained. Cost $3.06.

New York City (Cont.)

Records from May 13, 1943, to date: City Clerk's Office in borough in which license was issued. Cost $3.06.

The cost of $3.06 on the above is when the exact year if marriage is submitted. Ad $0.50 for 2nd year search and $0.25 for each additional year. Certificates will show names, ages, dates of birth, and date of marriage.

Bronx Borough

Office of City Clerk, 1780 Grand Concourse, Bronx, New York 10457. Records for 1908-1913 for Bronx are filed in Manhattan Office.

Brooklyn Borough

Office of City Clerk, Municipal Building, Brookln, New York 11201.

Manhattan Borough

Office of City Clerk, Municipal Building, New York, New York 10007.

Queens Borough

Office of City Clerk, 120-55 Queens Boulevard, Borough Hall Station, Jamaica, New York 11424.

Richmond Borough

Office of City Clerk, Borough Hall, St. George, Staten Island, New York 10301.

NORTH CAROLINA

Records since January 1, 1962: Public Health Statistics Section, State Board of Health, P.O. Box 2091, Raleigh, North Carolina 27602. Cost $2.00.

Register of Deeds in county where marriage was performed. Cost varies.

NORTH DAKOTA

Records since July 1, 1925: Division of Vital Statistics, State Department of Health, Bismarck, North Dakota 58501. Inquires will be forwarded to appropriate office. Certified copies are not available from State health department.

County Judge in county where license was issued. Cost varies.

OHIO

Records since September, 1949: Division of Vital Statistics, State Department of Health, G-20 State Department Building, Columbus, Ohio 43215. Inquiries will be forwarded to the appropriate office. All items may be verified, however, certified copies are not available from State health department.

Probate Judge in county where license was issued. Cost $1.00.

OKLAHOMA

Clerk of Court in county where license was issued. Cost varies.

OREGON

Records since January 1907: Vital Statistics Section, State Board of Health, P.O. Box 231, Portland, Oregon 97207. Cost $2.00.

County Clerk of County where license was issued. Cost varies.

PENNSYLVANIA

Records since January 1941: Division of Vital Statistics, State Department of Health, Health and Welfare Building, P.O. Box 90, Harrisburg, Pennsylvania 17120. Inquiries will be forwarded to the appropriate office. Certified copies are not available from State health department.

Marriage License Clerks, County Court House in county where license was issued.

PUERTO RICO

Division of Demographic Registry and Vital Statistics, Department of Health, San Juan, Puerto Rico 00908. Cost $0.50.

RHODE ISLAND

Records since January 1853: Division of Vital Statistics, Rhode Island Department of Health, Room 353, State Office Building, Providence, Rhode Island 02903. Cost $1.00.

Town Clerk in town, or City Clerk in City, where marriage was performed. Cost $1.00.

SOUTH CAROLINA

Records since July 1, 1950: Bureau of Vital Statistics, State Board of Health, Sims Building, Columbia, South Carolina 29201. Cost $2.00.

Records since July 1, 1911: Probate Judge in county where license was issued. Cost varies.

SOUTH DAKOTA

Records since July 1, 1905: Division of Public Health Statistics, State Department of Health, Pierre, South Dakota 57501. Cost $2.00.

Clerk of Courts in county where license was issued. Cost $2.00.

TENNESSEE

Records since July 1945: Division of Vital Records, State Department of Public Health, Cordell Hull Building, Nashville, Tennessee 37219. Cost $2.00

County Court Clerk in county where license was issued. Cost varies.

TEXAS

County Clerk in county where license was issued. Cost varies.

TRUST TERRITORY OF THE PACIFIC ISLANDS

Clerk of Court in district where marriage was performed. Cost varies.

UTAH

County Clerk in county where license was issued. Cost varies.

VERMONT

Records since 1857: Secretary of State, Vital Records Department, State House, Montpelier, Vermont 05602. Cost $1.50.

Town Clerk in town where license was issued. Cost $1.00.

VIRGINIA

Records since January 1853: Bureau of Vital Records and Health Statistics, State Department of Health, James Mad-

106

VIRGINIA CONT.

ison Building, P.O. Box 1000, Richmond, Virginia 23208.
Cost $2.00.

County Clerk in county or city where license was issued.
Cost varies

VIRGIN ISLANDS

Bureau of Vital Records and Statistical Services, Virgin
Islands Department of Health, Charlotte Amalie, St. Thomas, Virgin Islands 00801. Inquires will be forwarded
to the appropriate office. Certified copies are not
available form State health department.

St. Croix

Clerk of Municipal Court, Municipal Court of the Virgin
Islands, Christiansted, St. Croix, Virgin Island 00820.
Cost $0.50.

St. Thomas & St. John

Clerk of Municipal Court, Municipal Court of the Virgin
Islands, Charlotte Amalie, St. Thomas 00801. Cost $0.50.

WASHINGTON

Records since January 1, 1968: Bureau of Vital Statistics,
Division of Health, Washington State Department of Social
and Health Services, Olympia, Washington 98501. Cost $3.00.

County Auditor in county where license was issued. Cost
$2.00

WEST VIRGINIA

Records since 1921: Division of Vital Statistics, State
Department of Health, Charleston, West Virginia 25311.
Inquiries will be forwarded to the appropriate office.
Some items may be varified for $1.00.

County Clerk in county where license was issued. Cost
varies.

WISCONSIN

Records since April 1835: Bureau of Health Statistics,
Wisconsin Division of Health, P.O. Box 309, Madison. Wisconsin 53701. Cost $2.00.

WYOMING

Records since May 1941: Vital Records Services, Division of Health and Medical Services, State Office Building, Cheyenne, Wyoming 82001. Cost $2.00.

County Clerk in county where license was issued. Cost varies.

(Note: The data for this section on marriage records was provided by Joseph Alercia, II).

19. DIVORCE RECORDS

An official record of every divorce or annulment or marriage should be available in the place where the event took place. These records may be filed permanently either in a State vital statistics office or in a city, county, or other local office. When writing for a copy it is suggested that a money order or certified check be enclosed since the office cannot refund cash lost in transit. The following information will assist in locating the information you request:

1. Full names of husband and wife.
2. Present residence address.
3. Former addresses (as in court records)
4. Ages at time of divorce (or dates of birth).
5. Date and place of divorce or annulment of marriage.

A copy may be obtained by writing to the appropriate office listed below. Fees listed are subject to change.

ALABAMA

Records since January 1950: Bureau of Vital Statistics, State Department of Public Health, Montgomery, Alabama 36104. $2.00 fee includes search and report, or copy if found.

Clerk or Registrar of Court of Equity in county where divorce was granted.

ALASKA

Records since 1950: Bureau of Vital Statistics, Department of Health and Welfare, Pouch "H", Juneau, Alaska 99801. Cost $2.00.

Clerk of the Superior Court in judicial district where divorce was granted: Jeneau and Ketchikan (First District), Nome (Second District), Anchorage (Third District), Fairbanks (Fourth District), Alaska. Cost varies.

AMERICAN SAMOA

Registrar of Vital Statistics, Pago Pago, American Samoa, 96920. Cost $1.00.

ARIZONA

Clerk of Superior Court in county where divorce was granted. Cost varies.

ARKANSAS

Records since 1923: Bureau of Vital Statistics, State Department of Health, Little Rock, Arkansas 72201. Cost $2.00.

Clerk of Circuit or Chancery Court on county where divorce was granted. Cost varies.

CALIFORNIA

For final decree entered since January 1, 1962 or intial complaint filed since January 1, 1966: Bureau of Vital Statistics, Department of Public Health, 1927 13th Street, Sacramento, California 95814. Cost $2.00.

Clerk of Superior Court in county where divorce was granted. Cost varies.

CANAL ZONE

Balboa Division (Pacific Area), Clerk, U.S. District Court, Box 2006, Balboa Heights, Canal Zone. Cost varies.

Cristobal Division (Atlantic Area), Clerk, U.S. District Court, Box 1175, Cristobal, Canal Zone.

COLORADO

Statewide index of records for all years except 1940-1967: Records and Statistics Section, Colorado Department of Health, 4210 East 11th Avenue, Denver, Colorado 80220. Inquiries will be forwarded to appropriate county office. Certified copies not available.

Clerk of District Court, or Clerk of County Court, in county where divorce was granted. Cost varies.

CONNECTICUT

Index of records since June 1, 1947: Public Health Statistics Section, State Department of Health, 79 Elm Street, Hartford, Connecticut 06115. Inquiries will be forwarded to appropriate office. Certified copies not available.

CONNECTICUT CONT.

Clerk of Superior Court in county where divorce was granted. Cost $3.00.

DELAWARE

Records since March 1932, Bureau of Vital Statistics State
Board of Health, Dover, Delaware 19901. Inquiries will be
forwarded to appropriate office. Some items may be verified for $1.00.

Prothonotary in county where divorce was granted. Cost
$2.00.

DISTRICT OF COLUMBIA

Records since September 16, 1956: Clerk of District of Columbia Court of General Sessions, Washington, D.C. 20001.
Cost varies.

Records prior to September 16, 1956: Clerk, U.S. District
Court for the District for the District of Colubia, Washington, D.C. 20001. Cost varies.

FLORIDA

Records since June 6, 1927: Bureau of Vital Statistics,
State Board of Health, P.O. Box 210, Jacksonville, Florida
32201. If year is unknown, the fee is $2.00 for the first
year searched and $1.00 for each additional year to a maxi-
mum of $25.00. Fee includes a copy of the record if found.

Clerk of Circuit Court in county where divorce was granted.
Cost varies.

GEORGIA

Records since June 9, 1952: Vital Records Service, State
Department of Public Health, 47 Trinity Avenue, S.W., Atlanta Georgia 30334. Inquiries will be forwarded to appropriate office. All items may be verified but certified copies
not available.

Clerk of Superior Court in county where divorce was granted. Cost varies.

GUAM

Clerk, Island Court of Guam, Agana, Guam, M.I. 96910. Cost
varies.

HAWAII

Records since July 1, 1951: Research and Statistics Office, State Department of Health, P.O. Box 3378, Honolulu, Hawaii 96801. Cost $2.00.

Circuit Court in county where divorce was granted. Cost varies.

IDAHO

Records since January 1947: Bureau of Vital Statistics, State Department of Health, Boise, Idaho 83701. Cost $1.00.

County Recorder in county where divorce was granted. Cost varies.

ILLINOIS

Records since January 1, 1962: Bureau of Statistics, State Department of Public Health, Sprigfield, Illinois 62706. Some items may be verified for $2.00.

Clerk of Circuit Court in county where divorce was granted. Cost varies.

INDIANA

County Clerk in county where divorce was granted. Cost varies.

IOWA

Records since July 1906: Division of Records and Statistics, State Department of Health, Des Moines, Iowa 50319. Cost $1.00.

County Clerk in county where divorce was granted. Cost varies.

KANSAS

Records since July 1951: Division of Vital Statistics, State Department of Health, Topeka, Kansas 66612. Cost $2.00.

Clerk of District Court where divorce was granted. Cost varies.

KENTUCKY

Records since July 1, 1958: Office of Vital Statistics, State Department of Health, 275 East Main Street, Frankfort, Kentucky 40601. Cost $2.00.

KENTUCKY CONT.

Clerk of Circuit Court in county where divorce was granted. Cost varies.

LOUISIANA

Records since 1946: Division of Public Health Statistics, State Board of Health, P.O. Box 60630, New Orleans, Louisiana 70160. Inquiries will be forwarded to appropriate office. All items may be verified, however, certified copies are not available.

Clerk of Court in parish where divorce was granted. Cost varies.

MAINE

Records since January 1, 1892: Office of Vital Statistics, State Department of Health and Welfare, State House, Augusta, Maine 04330. Cost $2.00.

Clerk of Superior Court in county where divorce was granted or Clerk of District Court in the judicial division where divorce was granted. Cost $1.00.

MARYLAND

Records since January 1961: Division of Vital Records, State Department of Health, State Office Building, 301 West Preston Street, Baltimore, Maryland 21201. Inquiries will be forwarded to appropriate office. Some items may be verified, however, certified copies not available.

Clerk of the Circuit Court in county where divorce was granted. Cost $1.50.

MASSACHUSETTS

Records since 1952: State Registrar of Vital Statistics, 272 State House, Boston, Massachusetts 02133. Inquirer will be directed where to forward request. Cost $1.50.

Clerk of Superior Court or Registrar of Probate Court in county where divorce was granted. Cost $1.50.

MICHIGAN

Records since 1897: Vital Records Section, Michigan Department of Health, 3500 North Logan Street, Lansing, Michigan 48914. Cost $2.00.

County Clerk in county where divorce was granted. Cost varies.

MINNESOTA

Clerk of District Court in county where divorce was granted. Cost varies.

MISSISSIPPI

Records since January 1, 1926: Division of Public Health Statistics, State Board of Health, P.O. Box 1700, Jackson, Mississippi 39205. Inquiries will be forwarded to appropriate office. Certified copies not available.

Chancery Clerk in county where divorce was granted. Cost $1.00.

MISSOURI

Records since July 1948: Vital Records, Division of Health, State Department of Public Health and Welfare, Jefferson City, Missouri 65102. Inquiries will be forwarded to appropriate office. Some items may be verified.

Clerk of Circuit Court in county where divorce was granted. Cost varies.

MONTANA

Records since July 1943: Division of Records and Statistics, State Department of Health, Helena, Montana 59601. Inquiries will be forwarded to appropriate office. Some items may be verified.

Clerk of District Court in county where divorce was granted. Cost varies

NEBRASKA

Records since January 1909: Bureau of Vital Statistics, State Department of Health, State Capitol, Lincoln, Nebraska 68509. Cost $2.00.

Clerk of District Court where divorce was granted. Cost varies.

NEVADA

Records since January 1, 1968: Department of Health and Welfare, Division of Health, Section of Vital Statistics, Carson City, Nevada 89701. Cost $2.00.

County Clerk in county where divorce was granted. Cost varies.

NEW HAMPSHIRE

Records since 1880: Department of Health and Welfare, Division of Public Health, Bureau of Vital Statistics, 61 South Spring Street, Concord, New Hampshire 03301. $1.00 fee includes search and one copy.

Clerk of the Superior Court which issued the decree. Cost varies.

NEW JERSEY

Superior Court, Chancery Division, State House, Trenton, New Jersey 08625. Cost $2.00.

NEW MEXICO

Clerk of District Court in county where divorce was granted. Cost varies.

NEW YORK

Records since January 1, 1963: Office of Vital Records, State Department of Health, Albany, New York 12208. Cost $2.00.

County Clerk in county where divorce was granted. Cost varies.

NORTH CAROLINA

Records since January 1, 1958: Public Health Statistics Section, State Board of Health, P.O. Box 2091, Raleigh, North Carolina 27602. Cost $2.00.

Clerk of Superior Court in county where divorce was granted. Cost varies.

NORTH DAKOTA

Index of records since July 1, 1949: Division of Vital Statistics, State Department of Health, Bismarck, North Dakota 58501. Inquiries will be forwarded to appropriate office. Some items may be verified, however, certified copies not available.

Clerk of District Court in county where divorce was granted. Cost varies.

OHIO

Records since 1948: Division of Vital Statistics, State Department of Health, G-20 State Department Building, Co-

OHIO CONT.

lumbus, Ohio 43215. Inquiries will be forwarded to the appropriate office. All items may be verified, however, certified copies not available.

Clerk of Court of Common Pleas in county where divorce was granted. Cost $1.00.

OKLAHOMA

County Clerk in County where divorce was granted. Cost varies.

OREGON

Records since May 1925: Vital Statistice Section, State Board of Health, P.O. Box 231, Portland, Oregon 97207. Cost $2.00.

County Clerk in county where divorce was granted. Cost varies.

PENNSYLVANIA

Records since January 1946: Division of Vital Statistics, State Department of Health, Health and Welfare Building, P.O. Box 90, Harrisburg, Pennsylvania 17120. Inquiries will be forwarded to appropriate office, however, certified copies are not available.

Prothonotary, Court House, in county seat where divorce was granted. Cost varies.

PUERTO RICO

Superior Court where divorce was granted. Cost $0.60.

RHODE ISLAND

Records since January 1962: Division of Vital Statistics Rhode Island Department of Health, Room 353, State Office Building, Providence, Rhode Island 02903. Inquiries will be forwarded to appropriate office, however, certified copies are not available.

Clerk of Family Court in county where divorce was granted. Cost $1.00.

SOUTH CAROLINA

Records since July 1, 1962: Bureau of Vital Statistics, State Board of Health, Sims Building, Colubia, South Carolina 29201. Cost $1.00.

SOUTH CAROLINA CONT.

Records since 1949: Clerk of county where petition was filed. Cost varies.

SOUTH DAKOTA

Records since July 1, 1905: Division of Public Health Statistics, State Department of Health, Pierre, South Dakota 57501. Cost $2.00.

Clerk of Court in county where divorce was granted. Cost varies.

TENNESSEE

Records since July 1945: Division of Vital Statistics, State Department of Public Health, Cordell Hull Building. Nashville, Tennessee 37219.

Clerk of Court where divorce was granted. Cost varies.

TEXAS

Clerk of District Court in county where divorce was granted. Cost varies.

TRUST TERRITORY OF THE PACIFIC ISLANDS

Clerk of Court in District where divorce was granted. Cost varies.

UTAH

Records since 1958: Division of Vital Statistics, Utah State Department of Health, 44 Medical Drive, Salt Lake City, Utah 84113. Inquiries will be forwarded to the appropriate office. Some items may be verified, however, certified copies are not available.

Clerk of District Court in county where divorce was granted. Cost varies.

VERMONT

Records since January 1860: Secretary of State, Vital Records Department, State House, Montpelier, Vermont 05602. Cost $1.50.

Clerk of County Court where divorce was granted. Cost $3.00.

VIRGINIA

Records since January 1918: Bureau of Vital Records and

VIRGINIA CONT.

Health Statistics, State Department of Health, James Madison Building, P.O. Box 1000, Richmond, Virginia 23208. Cost $1.00.

Clerk of Court in county or city where divorce was granted. Cost varies.

VIRGIN ISLANDS

St. Croix

Deputy Clerk of District Court, Christiansted, St. Croix, Virgin Islands 00820. Cost $2.40.

St. Thomas & St. John

Clerk of District Court, Charlotte Amalie, St. Thomas, Virgin Islands 00802. Cost $2.40.

WASHINGTON

Records since January 1, 1968: Bureau of Vital Statistics, State Department of Health, Olympia, Washington 98501. Cost $2.00.

County Clerk in county where divorce was garnted. Cost varies.

WEST VIRGINIA

Clerk of Circuit Court, Chancery Side, in county where divorce was granted. Cost varies.

WISCINSIN

Records since October 1, 1907: Bureau of Health Statistics, Wisconsin Division of Health, P.O. Box 309, Madison, Wisconsin 53701. Cost $2.00.

WYOMING

Records since May 1941: Division of Vital Statistics, State Department of Public Health, Cheyenne, Wyoming 82001.

Clerk of District Court in county where divorce was granted. Cost varies.

(Note: The data for this section on divorce records was provided by Joseph Alercia, II).

20. BIRTH AND DEATH RECORDS

For every birth and death, an official certificate should be on file in the place where the event occurs. These certificates are prepared by physicians, funeral directors, other professional attendants, or hospital authorities. The Federal Government does not maintain files or indexes of these records. They are permanently filed in the central vital statistics office of the State, independent city, or outlying area where the event occurred. In writing for a certified copy, it is suggested that a money order or certified check be enclosed since the office cannot refund cash lost in transit. The letter of request should give the following facts:

1. Full name of the person whose record is being requested.
2. Sex and race.
3. Parents' names, including maiden name of mother.
4. Month, day, and year of the birth or death.
5. Place of birth or death (city or town, county, state, and name of hospital, if any).
6. Purpose for which copy is requested.
7. Relationship to person whose record is being requested.

To obtain a certified copy of a certificate, write or go to the vital statistics office in the State or area where the birth or death occured. The offices are listed below. Fees listed are subject to change.

ALABAMA

Bureau of Vital Statistics, State Department of Public Health, Montgomery, Alabama 36104. Cost for copy $2.00. Additional copies at same time are $1.00 each. State office has records since January 1, 1908. Fee for special searches is $3.00 per hour. Short forms or birth cards are not issued.

ALASKA

Bureau of Vital Statistics, Department of Health and Welfare, Pouch "H", Juneau, Alaska 99801. Cost of copy $2.00. State office has records since 1913. Cost of short form or birth card $2.00.

AMERICAN SAMOA

Office of the Territorial Registrar, Government of American Samoa, Pago Pago, American Samoa 96920. Cost of copy $1.00. Registrar has records on file since before 1900. Short forms or birth cards are not issue.

ARIZONA

Division of Vital Records, State Department of Health, P.O. Box 3887, Phoenix, Arizona 85030. Cost of copy $2.00. State office has records since July 1, 1909, and abstracts of records filed in the counties before that date. Cost of short form or birth card $2.00.

ARKANSAS

Bureau of Vital Statistics, State Department of Health, Little Rock, Arkansas 72201. Cost of copy $2.00. State office has records since February 1. 1914, as well as some original Little Rock and Fort Smith records from 1881. Short forms or birth cards are not issued.

CALIFORNIA

Bureau of Vital Statistics Registration, State Department of Health, 744 P. Street, Sacramento, California 95814. Cost of copy $2.00. State office has records since July 1, 1905. For records before that date, write to county Recorder in county of event. Cost of short form or birth card $2.00.

CANAL ZONE

Vital Statistics Clerk, Health Bureau, Balboa Heights, Canal Zone. Copies not issued. Central office has records since May 1904. Cost of short form or birth card $1.00.

COLORADO

Records and Statistics Section, Colorado Department of Health, 4210 East 11th Avenue, Denver, Colorado 80220. Cost of copy $2.00. State office has death records since 1900 and birth records since 1910. State office also has birth records for some counties for years prior to 1910. $2.00 fee is for search of files and one copy of record if found. Cost of short form or birth card $2.00.

CONNECTICUT

Public Health Statistics Section, State Department of Health, 79 Elm Street, Hartford, Connecticut 06115. Cost for copy $2.00. State office has records since July 1, 1897. For records before that date write to Registrar of Vital Statistics in town or city where birth or death occurred. Cost of short form or birth card $1.00.

DELAWARE

Bureau of Vital Statistics, Division of Physical Health,

DELAWARE CONT.

Department of Health and Social Services, Jesse S. Cooper Memorial Building, Dover, Delaware 19901. Cost of copy $2.50. State office has records for 1861 to 1863 and since 1881, but no records for 1864 through 1880. Cost of short form or birth card $2.50.

DISTRICT OF COLUMBIA

D.C. Department of Public Health, Vital Records Division, Room 1022, 300 Indiana Avenue, N.W., Washington, D.C. 20001. Cost of copy $1.00. Death records on file beginning with 1871, but no death records were filed during the Civil War. Cost of short form or birth card $1.00.

FLORIDA

Department of Health and Rehabilitative Services, Division of Health, Bureau of Vital Statistics, P.O. Box 210, Jacksonville, Florida 32201. Cost of copy $2.00. State office has some birth records since April 1865 and some death records since August 1877. The majority of records date from January 1917. Cost of copy $2.00. If the exact date is unknown and more than 1 year has to be searched, the fee is $2.00 for the first year searched and $1.00 for each additional year searched up to a maximum of $25.00. Fee includes a copy of the record if found. Cost of short form or birth card $2.00.

GEORGIA

Vital Records Service, State Department of Public Health, 47 Trinity Avenue, S.W., Atlanta, Georgia 30334. Cost of copy $3.00. Additional copies of same record ordered at same time are $1.00 each. The state office has records since January 1, 1919. For records before that date in Atlanta or Savannah, write to the County Health Department in the place where birth or death occurred. Cost of Short form or birth card $3.00.

GUAM

Office of Vital Statistics, Department of Public Health and Social Services, Government of Guam, P.O. Box 2816, Agana, Guam, M.I. 96910. Cost of copy $1.00. Office has records on file since October 26, 1901. Cost of Short form or birth card $1.00.

HAWAII

Research and Statistics Office, State Department of Health, P.O. Box 3378, Honolulu, Hawaii 96801. Cost of Copy $2.00. State office records since 1853. Cost of short form or birth card $2.00.

IDAHO

Bureau of Vital Statistics, State Department of Health, State House, Boise, Idaho 83707. Cost of copy $2.00. State office has records since 1911. For records from 1907 to 1911, write to County Recorder in county where birth or death occurred. Cost of short form or birth card $2.00.

ILLINOIS

Office of Vital Records, State Department of Public Health, 535 W. Jefferson Street, Springfield, Illinois, 62706. Cost of copy $2.00. This fee is for search of files and one copy of the record if found. Additional copies of the same record ordered at the same time are $1.00 each. The State office has records filed since January 1, 1916. For records filed before that date and for copies of State records since January 1, 1916, write to the County Clerk in the county where the birth or death occurred. Cost of short form or birth card $2.00.

INDIANA

Division of Vital Records, State Board of Health, 1330 West Michigan Street, Indianapolis, Indiana 46206. Cost of copy $3.00. Additional copies of the same record ordered at the same time are $1.00 each. State office has birth records since October 1, 1907, and death records since 1900. For records before that date, write to Health Officer in city or county where birth or death occurred. Short forms or birth cards are not issued.

IOWA

Division of Records and Statistics, State Department of Health, Des Moines, Iowa 50319. Cost of copy $2.00. State office has records since July 1, 1880.

KANSAS

Division of Registration and Health Statistics, 535 Kansas Avenue, Topeka, Kansas 66603. Cost of copy $2.00. State office has records since July 1, 1911. For records before that date, write to county clerk in county where birth or death occurred. Cost of shorth form or birth card $2.00.

KENTUCKY

Office of Vital Statistics, State Department of Health, 275 East Main Street, Frankfort, Kentucky 40601. Cost of copy $2.00. State office has records since January 1, 1911, and for Louisville and Lexington before that date.

KENTUCKY CONT.

If birth or death occurred in Covington before 1911, write
to City Health Department. Cost of short form or birth
card $2.00.

LOUISIANA (Except New Orleans)

Division of Public Health Statistics, State Department of
Health, P.O. Box 60630, New Orleans, Louisiana 70160. Cost
of copy $2.00. State office has records since July 1,
1914. Cost of short form or birth card $2.00.

New Orleans

Bureau of Vital Statistics, City Health Department, 1W03
City Hall Civic Center, New Orleans, Louisiana 70112. Cost
of copy $2.00. City Health Department has birth records
since 1790 and death records since 1803. Cost for short
form or birth card $2.00.

MISSISSIPPI

Vital Records Registration Unit, State Board of Health,
P.O. Box 1700, Jackson, Mississippi 39205. Cost of copy
$2.00. Shorth forms or birth cards not issued.

MISSOURI

Bureau of Vital Records, Division of Health, State Department of Public Health and Welfare, Jefferson City, Missouri 65101. Cost of copy $1.00. State office has records
beginning with January 1910. If birth or death occurred
in St. Louis (city), St. Louis County, or Kansas City before 1910, write to the City or County Health Department;
copies of these records are $2.00 each. Cost of short
form or birth card $1.00.

MONTANA

Bureau of Records and Statistics, State Department of Health
and Environmental Sciences, Helena 59601. Cost of copy
$2.00. State office has records since late 1907. Cost of
short form or birth card $2.00.

NEBRASKA

Bureau of Vital Statistics, State Department of Health, Lincoln Building, 1003 "O" Street, Lincoln, Nebraska 68508.
Cost of copy $2.00. State office has records since late
1904. If birth occurred before that date, write the State
office for information. Cost of short form or birth card
$2.00.

NEVADA

Department of Health, Welfare and Rehabilitation, Division of Health, Section of Vital Statistics, Carson City, Nevada 89701. Cost of copy $2.00. State office has records since July 1, 1911. For earlier records, write to County Recorder in county where birth or death occurred. Cost of short form or birth card $1.00.

NEW HAMPSHIRE

State Department of Health and Welfare, Division of Public Health, Bureau of Vital Statistics, 61 South Spring Street Concord, New Hampshire 03301. Cost of copy $1.00 which is for search of files and copy of record if found. Copies of records may be obtained from State office or firm from City or Town Clerk where birth or death occurred. Cost of short form or birth card $1.00.

NEW JERSEY

State Department of Health, Bureau of Vital Statistics, Box 1540, Trenton, New Jersey 08625. Cost of copy $2.00, which is for search of files and one copy of the record if found. Additional copies of same record ordered at the same time are $1.00 each. When the exact date is unknown the fee is an additional $0.50 per year searched. State office has records since June 1878. For records from May 1848 through May 1878, write State department of Education. Cost of short form or birth card $2.00.

MAINE

Office of Vital Records, State Department of Health and Welfare, State House, Augusta, Maine 04330. Cost of copy $1.00. State office has records since 1892. For records before that year, write to Town Clerk where birth or death occurred. Cost for short form or birth card $1.00.

MARYLAND

Division of Vital Records, State Department of Health, State Office Building, 301 West Preston Street, Baltimore, Maryland 21201. Cost of copy $2.00. State office has records since 1898. Cost of short form or birth card $2.00.

MASSACHUSETTS

Registrar of Vital Statistics, 272 State House, Boston, Massachusetts 02133. Cost of copy $1.00. State office has records since 1841. For records prior to that year, write to the City or Town Clerk in place where birth or death occurred. Earliest Boston records available in this office are for 1848. Short form or birth card are free.

MICHIGAN

Vital Records Section, Michigan Department of Public Health, 3500 North Logan Street, Lansing, Michigan 48914. Cost of copy $2.00. State office has records since 1867. Copies of records since 1867 may also be obtained from County Clerk. Detroit Records may be obtained from the City Health Department for births occurring since 1893 and for deaths since 1897. Cost of short form or birth card $2.00.

MINNESOTA

Minnesota Department of Health, Section of Vital Statistics, 717 Delaware Street, S.E., Minneapolis, Minnesota 55440. Cost of copy $2.00. State office has records since January 1908. Copies of records prior to 1908 may be obtained from Clerk of District Court in county where birth or death occurred or from the Minneapolis or St. Paul City Health Department if the event occurred in either city. Cost of short form or birth card $2.00.

NEW MEXICO

Vital Records, New Mexico Health and Social Services Department, PERA Building, Room 118, Santa Fe, New Mexico 87501. Cost of copy $1.00. All records in State office. Short form or birth card not issued.

NEW YORK (Except N.Y. City)

Bureau of Vital Records, State Department of Health, Albany, New York 12208. Cost of Copy $2.00. State office has records since 1880. For records prior to !914 in Albany, Buffalo, and Yonkers or before 1880 in any other city, write to Registrar of Vital Statistics in the city where birth or death occurred. For the rest of the State except New York City, write to the State office. Cost of short form or birth card $2.00.

NEW YORK CITY

Bronx Borough

Bureau of Records and Statistics, Department of Health of New York City, 1826 Arthur Avenue, Bronx, New York 10457. Cost of copy $2.50. Additional copies of same record ordered at the same time are $1.25 each. Records on file since 1898. Records from 1866 to 1897 on file in Manhattan Borough. Cost of short form or birth card $2.50.

Brooklyn Borough

County Clerk, Kings County, Historical Division, 360 Adams Street, Brooklyn, New York 11201. Cost of copy $2.50.

Brooklyn Borough Cont.

Records for deaths on file from 1847 to 1865. Short forms or birth cards not issued.

Bureau of Records and Statistics, Department of Health of New York City, 295 Flatbush Avenue Ext., Brooklyn, New York 11201. Cost of Copy $2.50. Additional copies of the same record at the same time are $1.25 each. Records on file since 1866. Cost of short form or birth card $2.50.

Manhattan Borough

Bureau of Records and Statistics, Department of Health of New York City, 125 Worth Street, New York, New York 10013. Cost of Copy $2.50. Additional copies of same record ordered at the same time are $1.25 each. Records on file since 1866. For Old City of New York (Manhattan and part of the Bronx) death records from 1847 to 1865, write to Municipal Archives and Records Retention Center of the New York Public Library, 238 William Street, New York, New York 10038. Cost of short form or birth card $2.50.

Queens Borough

Bureau of Records and Statistics, Department of Health of New York City, 90-37 Parsons Boulevard, Jamaica, New York 11432. Cost of copy $2.50. Additional copies of same record ordered at the same time are $1.25 each. Records on file since 1898. Records prior to that year are on file with State Department of Health. Cost of short form or birth card $2.50.

Richmond Borough

Bureau of Records and Statistics, Department of Health of New York City, 51 Stuyvesant Place, St. George, Staten Island, New York 10301. Cost of copy $2.50. Additional copies of same record ordered at the same time are $1.25 each. Records on file since 1898. Records prior to that year are on file with the State Department of Health. Cost of short form or birth card $2.50.

NORTH CAROLINA

Vital Records Section, State Board of Health, P.O.Box 2091 Raleigh, North Carolina 27602. Cost of copy $2.00. State office has records since October 1, 1913, and some delayed records prior to that date. Cost of short form or birth card $2.00.

NORTH DAKOTA

Division of Vital Statistics, State Department of Health, Bismarck, North Dakota 58501. Cost of copy $2.00. State office has some records from July 1, 1893; years from 1894 to 1920 are incomplete. Cost of short form or birth card $2.00.

OHIO

Division of Vital Statistics, State Department of Health, G-20 State Departments Building, Columbus, Ohio 43215. Cost of copy $1.00. State office has records since December 20, 1908. For records before that date write to Probate Court in county where birth or death occurred. Cost of short form or birth card $1.00.

OKLAHOMA

Vital Records Section, State Department of Health, 3400 North Eastern, Oklahoma City, Oklahoma 73105. Cost of copy $2.00. State office has records since October 1908. Cost of short form or birth card $2.00.

OREGON

Vital Statistics Section, Oregon State Health Division, P.O. Box 231, Portland, Oregon 97207. Cost of copy $3.00. Additional copies of the same record ordered at the same time are $2.00 each. State office has records since July 1903. State office has some earlier records for City of Portland dating from approximately 1880. Cost of short form or birth card $3.00.

PENNSYLVANIA

Division of Vital Statistics, State Department of Health, Health and Welfare Building, P.O. Box 90, Harrisburg, Pennsylvania 17120. Cost of copy $2.00. State office has records since January 1, 1906. For records before that date, write to Register of Wills, Orphans Court, county seat where birth or death occurred. Persons born in Pittsburg from 1870 to 1905 or in Allegheny City, now part of Pittsburg, from 1882 to 1905 should write to the Office of Biostatistics, Pittsburg Health Department, City-County Building, Pittsburg, Pennsylvania 15219. For births and deaths occurring in the City of Philadelphia from 1860 to 1915, apply to Vital Statistics, Philadelphia Department of Public Health, City Hall Annex, Philadelphia Pennsylvania 19107. Cost of short form or birth card $1.00.

PUERTO RICO

Division of Demographic Registry and Vital Statistics, Department of Health, San Juan, Puerto 00908. Cost of copy $0.50. Central office has records since July 22, 1931. Copies of records prior to that date may be obtained by writing to local Registrar (Registrador Demografico) in municipality where birth or death occurred or to central office. Cost of short form or birth card $0.50.

RHODE ISLAND

Division of Vital Statistics, State Department of Health, Room 101 Health Building, Davis Street, Providence, Rhode Island 02908. Cost of copy $1.00. State office has records since 1853. For records before that year, write to Town Clerk in town where birth or death occurred. Cost of short form or birth card $1.00.

SOUTH CAROLINA

Bureau of Vital Statistics, State Board of Health, Sims Building, Columbia, South Carolina 29201. Cost of copy $2.00. State office has records since January 1, 1915. City of Charleston births from 1877 and deaths from 1821 on file at Charleston County Health Department. Ledger entries of Florence City births and deaths from 1895 to 1914 on file at Florence County Health Department. Ledger entries of Newberry City births and deaths from late 1800's on file at Newberry County Health Department. Early records are obtainable only from County Health Departments listed. Cost of short form or birth card $2.00.

SOUTH DAKOTA

Division of Public Health Statistics, State Department of Health, Pierre, South Dakota 57501. Cost of copy $2.00. State office has records since July 1, 1905, and access to other records for some births and deaths which occurred before that date. Cost of short form or birth card $2.00.

TENNESSEE

Division of Vital Statistics, State Department of Public Health, Cordell Hull Building, Nashville, Tennessee 37219. Cost of copy $2.00. State office has birth records for entire State from January 1, 1914, to date and records from June 1881 for Nashville, July 1881 for Knoxville, and January 1882 for Chattanooga. State office has death records for entire State from January 1, 1914, to date and records from July 1874 for Nashville, March 6, 1872, for Chattanooga, and July 1, 1887, for Knoxville. Birth and death enumeration records by school districts from July 1,

TENNESSEE CONT.

1908, through June 30, 1912. Memphis birth records are from April 1, 1874, through December 1887; records continue November 1, 1898, to January 1, 1914. Death records date from May 1, 1848, to January 1, 1914. Apply to Memphis-Shelby County Health Department, Division of Vital Statistics, Memphis, Tennessee.

TEXAS

Bureau of Vital Statistics, State Department of Health, 410 East 5th Street, Austin, Texas 78701. Cost of copy $2.00. State office has records since 1903. Cost of short form or birth card $2.00.

UTAH

Division of Vital Statistics, Utah State Department of Health, 44 Medical Drive, Salt Lake City, 84113. Cost of copy $2.00. State office has records since 1905. If birth or death occurred from 1890 through 1904 in Salt Lake City or Ogden, write to City Board of Health. For records elsewhere in the State from 1898 through 1904, write to County Clerk in county where birth or death occurred. Cost of short form or birth card $2.00.

VERMONT

Town or City Clerk of town where birth or death occurred. Cost of copy $2.00. Cost of short form or birth card $1.00; Secretary of State, Vital Records Department, State House, Montpelier, Vermont 05602. Cost of copy or short form or birth card $1.50; Public Health Statistics Division, Department of Health, Burlington, Vermont 05401.

VIRGINIA

Bureau of Vital Records and Health Statistics, State Department of Health, James Madison Building, Box 1000, Richmond, Virginia 23208. Cost of copy $2.00. State office has records from January 1858 through December 1896 and since June 4, 1912. For records between those dates, write to the Health Department in the city where the birth or death occurred. Cost of short form or birth card $2.00.

VIRGIN ISLANDS

St. Thomas

Registrar of Vital Statistics, Charlotte Amalie, St. Thomas, Virgin Islands 00802. Cost of copy $2.00. Re-

St. Thomas Cont.

gistrar has birth records on file since July 1, 1906, and death records since January 1, 1906. Cost of short form or birth card $1.00.

St. Croix

Registrar of Vital Statistics, Charles Harwood Memorial Hospital, St. Croix, Virgin Islands. Cost of copy $1.00. Registrar has birth and death records on file since 1840. Cost of short form or birth card $1.00.

WASHINGTON

Bureau of Vital Statistics, Department of Health and Social Services, P.O. Box 709, Olympia, Washington 98504. Cost of copy $3.00. State office has records since July 1, 1907. In Seattle, Spokane, and Tacoma a copy may also be obtained from the City Health Department. For records before July 1, 1907, write to Auditor in county where birth or death occurred. Cost of short form or birth card $3.00.

WEST VIRGINIA

Division of Vital Statistics, State Department of Health, State Office Building No.3, Charleston, West Virginia 25305. Cost of copy $1.00. State office has records since January 1917. For records prior to that yaer, write to Clerk of County Court in the county where birth or death occurred. Short forms or birth cards not issued.

WISCONSIN

Bureau of Health Statistics, Wisconsin Division of Health, P.O. Box 309, Madison, Wisconsin 53701. State office has some records since 1814; early years are incomplete. Cost of copy or short form or birth card $2.00.

WYOMING

Vital Records Services, Division of Health and Medical Services, State Office Building, Cheyenne 82001. State office has records since July 1909. Cost of copy or short form or birth card $2.00.

INVESTIGATOR ASSOCIATIONS

By becoming a member of professional associations, an investigator can develop contacts all over the country, as well as around the world. Most states have a State Association which licensed investigators of that state can join. Investigators can often join other state organizations as an honorary or associate member.

The following are some associations that may be of interest to the private investigator. The listing of these organizations in no way implies endorsement or approval by the author or publisher.

1. ASSOCIATED LICENSED DETECTIVES OF NEW YORK STATE (ALDONYS)
   1806 East Avenue
   Rochester, NY 14610
   (716) 244-3400

2. ASSOCIATED SPECIAL INVESTIGATORS AND POLICE INTERNATIONAL, INC.
   International Headquarters
   P.O. Box 434
   Saint John, N.B.
   Canada, E2L-4L9

3. COUNCIL OF INTERNATIONAL INVESTIGATORS
   World Headquarters
   311 Oak Grove Drive
   P.O. Box 2712
   Akron, OH 44319
   (216) 644-2834

4. FLORIDA ASSOCIATION OF PRIVATE INVESTIGATORS, INC.
   Association Headquarters
   P.O. Box 2461
   Tampa, FL 33601
   (813) 879-8580

5. INTERNATIONAL ASSOCIATION OF ARSON INVESTIGATORS
   25 Newton Street
   P.O. Box 600
   Marlboro, MA 01752
   (617) 481-5977

6. INTERNATIONAL ASSOCIATION OF CHIEFS OF POLICE
   13 Firstfield Road
   Gaithersburg, MD 20878
   (301) 948-0922

7. INTERNATIONAL ASSOCIATION OF CREDIT CARD INVESTIGATORS
   1620 Grant Avenue
   Novato, CA 94947
   (415) 897-8800

8. INTERNATIONAL ASSOCIATION OF LAW ENFORCEMENT INTELLIGENCE
   ANALYSTS
   P.O. Box 876
   Ben Franklin Station
   Washington, DC 20044

9. INTERNATIONAL POLICE CONGRESS
   Regional Records Division
   8740 SW 158th Street
   P.O. Box 570552
   Miami, FL 33157
   (305) 238-1147

10. MICHIGAN ASSOCIATION OF PRIVATE DETECTIVES AND SECURITY
    AGENCIES, INC.
    P.O. Box 123
    Southfield, MI 48037
    (313) 476-7372

11. NATIONAL ASSOCIATION OF CHIEFS OF POLICE
    1000 Connecticut Avenue, NW
    Washington, DC 20036
    (202) 293-9088

12. NATIONAL COUNCIL OF INVESTIGATION AND SECURITY
    P.O. Box 433
    Severna Park, MD 21146
    (301) 261-1241

13. NATIONAL COUNCIL OF INVESTIGATION AND SECURITY SERVICES
    (NCISS)
    3625 Hauck Road
    Cincinatti, OH 45241
    (513) 554-0500

14. NATIONAL MILITARY INTELLIGENCE ASSOCIATION
    1608 Laurel Lane
    Annapolis, MD 21401

15. NEVADA ASSOCIATION OF INVESTIGATORS
    P.O. Box 1962
    Las Vegas, NV 89101

16. PRIVATE INVESTIGATORS ASSOCIATION OF VIRGINIA, INC.
    P.O. Box 7600
    Alexandria, VA 22307
    (703) 385-1333

17. SECURITY AND INTELLIGENCE FUND
    499 S Capitol Street, SW, Suite 500
    Washington, DC 20003

18. SOCIETY OF PROFESSIONAL INVESTIGATORS
    1120 E 31st Street
    Brooklyn, NY 11210

19. WORLD ASSOCIATION OF DETECTIVES
    P.O. Box 36174
    Cincinnati, OH 45236
    (513) 891-2002

CORRESPONDENCE SCHOOLS

Education is a very important aspect of every professionals career. The best education for any investigator is the apprenticeship mandated by most states. However, correspondence courses can be a means by which to learn the basics of investigation or test yourself on the knowledge which you may have become rusty on. The following is a list of correspondence schools available to persons desiring to learn the basics of investigation. The listing of these correspondence schools in no way implies endorsement or approval by the author or the publisher.

1. AMERICAN DETECTIVE INSTITUTE
   P.O. Box 418
   Fairfield, AL 35064

2. AMERICAN POLICE ACADEMY
   BASIC COURSE FOR PRIVATE INVESTIGATORS
   Suite 615, Headquarters Building
   2000 "P", Street NW
   Washington, DC 20036

3. GLOBAL SCHOOL OF INVESTIGATION
   Global, Box 191
   Hanover, MA 02339

4. LION INVESTIGATION ACADEMY
   3161 Shakespeare Road
   Bethlehem, PA 18017
   (215) 868-2637

5. POLICE SCIENCE INSTITUTE
   4400 Campus Drive
   Newport Beach, CA 92660

6. PROFESSIONAL INVESTIGATORS TRAINING SCHOOL
   P.O. Box 41345
   Los Angeles, CA 90041

7. THE INVESTIGATORS TRAINING ACADEMY
   1717 Montana Avenue
   El Paso, TX 79902

8. WESTERN COLLEGE OF CRIMINOLOGY
   18411 Crenshaw Boulevard
   Torrance, CA 90504

CODE OF ETHICS

1. As a private investigator, I regard myself as a member of a vital and honorable profession.

2. As a private investigator, I will strive to keep myself available to at least listen to the problems of any citizen who may seek my counsel. I will, at all times, attempt to either serve a client to the best of my own capabilities or I will refer him to someone known to me to be more capable than myself.

3. As a private investigator, I shall attempt to keep myself knowledgeable of the laws pertaining to my profession and to all other phases of public and private law enforcement agencies, and to abide by those laws explicitly at all times.

4. As a private investigator, I will maintain constant mindfulness that when I am on a case I am essentially a direct representative, an external and specialized agent of my client. My conduct will always be honorable and professional so as not to reflect in a negative way upon that client.

5. As a private investigator, my reports of progress will always be made to my client at the time and place and with the content and regularity that has previously been agreed upon.

6. As a private investigator, I shall attempt, at all times, to establish and maintain appropriate dialogue between myself and my client.

7. As a private investigator, I will always respect the wishes of my client - except in serious criminal findings, the nature of which I am legally bound to disclose to the appropriate law enforcement agency.

8. As a private Investigator, I will diligently pursue each and every assignment that I accept with interest and enthusiasm until a final and acceptable conclusion can be drawn to the mutual satisfaction of my client and myself.

9. As a private Investigator, I know that no one is more professionally important to me than my client. I will serve my client with honesty, integrity, loyalty and dispatch with legally proper and thoroughly dedicated, proficient and professional demeanor.

INDEX TO FORMS

1. Accident Case Report Outline 70

2. Agreement for Service 85

3. Application For Employment 9

4. Case Log Sheet 83

5. Case Work Sheet 86

6. Civil Litigation Information Sheet 43

7. Consent Form 46

8. Criminal Case Report Outline 72

9. Diagram Sheet 73

10. File Cards 84

11. Interview Guide 54

12. Missing Person Report 15

13. Original Case Notes 47

14. Outline for Report Coversheet 69

15. Photo Data Sheet 66

16. Photograph Mounting Form 74

17. Pretext Survey 8

18. Surveillance Report Outline 71